Other books by Chip Ingram

GOOD to GREAT in
God's Eyes

10 Practices Great Christians Have in Common

CHIP INGRAM

BakerBooks

Grand Rapids, Michigan

© 2007 by Chip Ingram

Published by Baker Books
a division of Baker Publishing Group
P.O. Box 6287, Grand Rapids, MI 49516-6287
www.bakerbooks.com

Published in association with Yates & Yates, LLP, Attorneys and Counselors, Orange, California.

Paperback edition published 2009
ISBN 978-0-8010-7214-7

Printed in the United States of America

The Library of Congress has cataloged the hardcover edition as follows:
Ingram, Chip, 1954–
    Good to great in God's eyes : 10 practices great Christians have in common / Chip Ingram.
        p.   cm.
    Includes bibliographical references.
    ISBN 10: 0-8010-1293-7 (cloth)
    ISBN 978-0-8010-1293-8 (cloth)
    ISBN 10: 0-8010-7052-X (intl. pbk.)
    ISBN 978-0-8010-7052-5 (intl. pbk.)
    1. Christian life. 2. Spiritual life—Christianity. I. Title.
BV4501.3.I53 2007
248.4—dc22   2007015771

Contents

Introduction

I couldn't sleep, so I stayed up half the night thinking about some questions that had been bothering me. Is it really wrong to want to be great? Is it self-centered to want your life to really make an impact? Does ambition indicate a spiritual problem? Am I "carnal" for thinking such things?

After tossing and turning for a couple of hours, I got up, made some hot tea, found my wife's rocking chair, and stared into the fireplace, mentally reviewing all the things God had been teaching me lately. One idea in particular seemed to capture my attention: what does "greatness" in God's kingdom look like?

I had recently spent some time in Luke 22, a passage that raises this question. Near the end of Jesus's earthly ministry, the disciples argued about which one of them was the greatest. Surprisingly, Jesus never rebuked them for their longing to be great. He gave them a completely new paradigm about what greatness is, but he didn't condemn their desire. I was intrigued by that.

I also had been reading *Good to Great*, Jim Collins's bestselling book about the practices of companies that are a cut above the rest.[1] Collins and his team thoroughly researched hundreds of businesses and came up with a list of characteristics that distinguish great companies from good or mediocre ones. It has become one of the most popular business leadership books of all time. I was fascinated by the idea that such a small handful of principles can make such a huge difference in success.

As I sat up that night with these thoughts turning over in my mind, I realized that greatness is nearly everyone's ambition in nearly every area of their lives. Corporate leaders want their companies to be great; professionals want to have great careers; men want to be great husbands and fathers, and women want to be great wives and mothers; athletes want to be great competitors; scholars want to be great thinkers and researchers; artists want to create great art; and on and on. Mediocrity is almost no one's ambition.

I've asked a lot of people about their hopes and dreams, and I usually get unapologetic answers about their desires to be great at what they do. But when I ask believers if they want to be great Christians, they seem to be afraid to answer the question. They become unassuming and deferential, concerned that an ambition to be great in this most important aspect of life would seem arrogant. To talk about ambition in following Christ sounds like the opposite of humble spiritual maturity.

Yet what's the alternative? Should we aspire to be mediocre Christians? Is it really prideful to want to honor God with lives of great faith and excellent work?

Even after spending three years with Jesus, the disciples didn't seem to think so. They argued about which one of them was the greatest, and though Jesus had to redefine greatness for them, he didn't tell them they were being unspiritual or arrogant because of their intense desire and ambition to be great. Instead he laid out a clear but counterintuitive pathway that eleven of the twelve eventually fulfilled. And their greatness, as they followed that pathway, turned the world upside down in less than a century.

As for Jesus himself, he didn't seem prone to mediocrity either, did he? In fact, in a long prayer the night before his crucifixion, he said to the Father: "I have brought you glory on earth by completing the work you gave me to do" (John 17:4). He went on to ask that the Father glorify him and that his glory be shared with his disciples. Those are bold statements about greatness, yet we would never accuse Jesus of being arrogant and immodest. His statements were true, and from God's perspective, his desires were godly.

God's perspective. That's the context that makes greatness a desirable quality. It's one thing to be great in terms of financial success or popular opinion; that's usually a self-centered, immodest ambition. But to be great in God's kingdom? That's a noble desire. We were *designed* to be great in God's eyes. When he created humanity, he proclaimed us not just good, but "very good" (Gen. 1:31). We exist for his glory. That kind of purpose isn't served well by mediocrity or even by settling for simply being good.

No, God loves it when his people are zealous about making a difference for his kingdom. He eagerly looks over the landscape of this world to honor, empower, and strengthen those whose love and obedience bring him pleasure. Our greatness—as he defines it—is his desire.

Over the last three or four years, I have been wrestling with this concept of greatness in God's eyes. How can we throw off false humility and fully embrace God-given desires and dreams that bring honor and glory to his name? In my journey, I've stayed up late, pondered, read, and—much like Jim Collins began to notice in his research with successful businesses—I've begun to observe that great Christians have certain practices in common. My research is less methodical and empirical than that of Collins and his team of researchers—after all, the complex characteristics of corporate culture are a little harder to discern than the practices of individual Christians. But as I have surveyed the lives of great men and women of faith, I have noticed certain patterns that I consider to be valid evidence of the difference between an ordinary and an extraordinary Christian life. When I see the practices identified in this book in a Christian's life, the result is almost always a rare level of maturity and fruitfulness. Conversely, when I *don't* see these practices in a person's life, the result is almost always mediocrity. This pattern flows out of numerous examples from Scripture, church history, and current experience. Christians who develop these practices with the right motivation are powerfully used by God for his glory.

Many people have projected into the future what they think their career ought to look like: a certain salary and position in five years, then in ten, then in twenty. Most of us have had similar projections for family: when we want to get married, how many children we want to have, where we want to live. Those timelines may not be written out; they may not even be conscious thoughts. But most of us have them, at least for those core areas of life that are important to us.

What would a spiritual timeline look like for you? What are your ambitions as a Christian? Have you thought about the kind of Christian you'd like to be in five, ten, and twenty years? Have you deeply pondered what kind of impact you want your life to have for Christ? What would your life look like if you, in fact, fulfilled Jesus's prayer that you "bear much fruit" (John 15:8)? What would the fruit look like? How would the world be different? When you have run the race with perseverance and finally cross the finish line, what kind of assessment of your life do you envision the Lord giving you?

There's nothing wrong with allowing yourself to think in those terms. In fact, Jesus's zeal for his Father's house consumed him (John 2:17). There's also nothing wrong with developing a plan to get there. Your plans must flow out of your God-given passions and your relationship with the Holy Spirit and his leading, but being sensitive to the Spirit does not rule out having a clear target for your discipleship.

In fact, a haphazard, go-with-the-flow approach will almost guarantee a mediocre spiritual life. In order for God to accomplish a great measure of his highest purposes for your life, you must give yourself permission to live out that passion with purpose and intentionality. Your faith can't be a random growth process. Proactive discipleship—longing to be great in God's eyes—will produce greater maturity and fruit than reactive discipleship. The Bible and experience are clear on that point. God urges us repeatedly in Scripture to be diligent about the disciplines and practices that lead to excellence, maturity, and impact.

I want to be clear about the specific role of these practices. They are by no means required for salvation. They will never earn you brownie points with God. They are no cause for spiritual pride, and they are not an obligation. This is not a ten-step plan to gain God's favor or to impress other people.

These principles are, however, an opportunity to fulfill the highest and best purposes God has for your life. Great athletes don't spend years practicing because they have to; they do it because they have a dream. Christians who want to live the average Christian life can do so, almost by default. None of the practices in this book are required for that. But those who dream of eternal impact in the kingdom of God, who envision crossing the finish line as one of God's great saints, are motivated to do whatever it takes to be used powerfully by God.

If you fit that description, the practical steps set forth in this book will help you attain a greater measure of Christlikeness and usefulness. If the honest desire of your heart is to stand before God one day and, like Jesus, tell him, "I have brought you glory on earth by completing the work you gave me to do" (John 17:4), these ten practices will make a huge difference in your life. They will put you on an uncommon path to greatness.

There are ten specific principles in this book, and though this list isn't exhaustive, it's quite thorough. You may think of another common denominator in the lives of great Christians or find a great Christian who didn't practice one or two of these principles. But in general, you'll find these patterns to be consistently present in the heroes of our faith. Consider them to be a reliable starting point, and cultivate them however God leads you to do so. Let them lead to a lifestyle of making more and more impact as a believer.

You will find at the end of each chapter an action plan to help you implement what you've learned. Because these chapters are about *practices*, it will probably be helpful to spend some time actually *practicing* each one before moving on to the next chapter. Remember that applying truth to your life is first a matter of quality; quantity comes second. God is not nearly as interested in your ability to learn truth as he is in your willingness to apply it. The action plans at the end of each chapter are designed to help you begin integrating what you've learned into your lifestyle.

God invites you to be a world-changing, kingdom-shaping Christian. The desire to be great was planted in your heart by the one who made you. But desires remain only desires if there's no follow-through, no plan to accomplish them. I hope and pray that this book will serve as a blueprint for building the life God has designed you for and fulfilling your highest desires. Most of all, I hope and pray that you will be fully satisfied in your quest to become great—in God's eyes.

1

Think Great Thoughts

Life consists of what a man is thinking about all day.

Ralph Waldo Emerson

The actions of men are the best interpreters of their thought.

John Locke

Nothing limits achievement like small thinking; nothing expands possibilities like unleashed thinking.

William Arthur Ward

You are today where your thoughts have brought you. You will be tomorrow where your thoughts take you.

James Allen

Dr. Jack Haskins, a professor at the University of Tennessee, spent twelve years researching the effects of media on how people think.[1] One of his studies attempted to determine the impact of a five-minute radio program that was filled with negative news stories: seventeen children blown up on a bus, an earthquake that killed thousands, riots in the streets of a large city, and so on. One group listened to negative programs like this daily, while a control group listened to more positive and uplifting news.

After evaluating the listeners who were daily exposed to five minutes of bad news, Haskins discovered four discernible effects on them: (1) they were more depressed than before; (2) they believed the world was a negative place; (3) they were less likely to help others; and (4) they began to believe that what they heard would soon happen to them. Simply by receiving and reflecting on the information from the radio program, their perceptions of the world and their outlook on life were adversely affected. Their concept of reality was shaped by their thoughts.

How could five minutes of negative thinking each day have that kind of influence? The old axiom, "You are what you eat," is true not only physically but also psychologically and spiritually. The thoughts we entertain in our minds become the thoughts that guide our lives, for better or for worse. And if five minutes can have such a dramatic impact, can you imagine what six or seven hours of TV every day does to someone's mind? The stream of negative news and skewed values that pours so freely into many of our minds clearly can change the way we live.

"As he thinketh in his heart, so is he," Proverbs 23:7 (KJV) tells us. When we put positive, winsome ideas into our minds—for example, "I am deeply loved by God," or "This is the day that the LORD has made; let us rejoice and be glad in it" (Ps. 118:24)—we have positive emotions. When we put discouraging, depressing ideas into our minds, we end up with negative emotions.

Whether we like it or not, what we think influences what we do. The thoughts we have, the feelings we feel, the experiences that shape our understanding—these things steer the ship of our lives. We act out of the perceptions we have, so those perceptions become a critical battleground.

Don't believe it? Just ask advertisers. Sales people know that once you are emotionally hooked on a car, a house, or anything else, your decision to buy will soon follow. The entire advertising industry is based on the fact that behavior flows out of whatever moods and thoughts we have, and everyone in the industry contends for them. So do politicians, philosophers, and preachers. We even try to influence ourselves.

Consciously we may trivialize the importance of our thoughts, but we obviously recognize their power. When we get depressed or anxious, we spend a lot of time, energy, and money on changing our emotions. We undergo counseling and take medications to get our moods and feelings back on course. We also spend a lot of time, energy, and money on fixing our behaviors. We turn to counseling, medication, accountability groups, training courses, and a number of other aids to control a habit or a personality flaw. But almost always, beneath the emotions we want to improve and the behavior we want to correct is a pattern of thinking that needs to change.

Picture a train, if you will. The engine is our thinking, and it pulls first the car of emotions, then the car of behavior, and then the car of consequences. Good thoughts will influence our emotions for good, which in turn will influence our behavior and produce positive consequences. Negative thoughts have the same influence in the opposite direction. What we think will determine the course of our life.

wrong thinking	→	negative emotions	→	unwise behavior	→	devastating consequences
right thinking	→	positive emotions	→	wise behavior	→	fruitful consequences

Great Christians think great thoughts. Augustine spent his academic life studying the works of great philosophers and conversing with the leading rhetoricians of his day. After he embraced the truth of the gospel, his well-trained mind turned its attention to eternal realities. His writings demonstrate a thought life constantly wrestling with lofty concepts and deep reflections. He has influenced Christian theology perhaps more than any post–New Testament figure because he thought great thoughts.

Centuries later, one of Augustine's admirers radically impacted Christian thought and helped spark the Protestant Reformation.

As a monk, Martin Luther spent long nights and anxious days deep in thought about the nature of salvation and the practices of the church. To a large degree, the Reformation in northern Europe was a product of his thought life. We still reap the benefits of this mind, which was long ago captivated by the deep things of God.

Augustine and Luther are just two examples among many— Blaise Pascal, C. S. Lewis, Francis Schaeffer, to name a few— whose thoughts have changed the course of history and enriched the Christian faith. And lest you think this practice applies only to the intellectual giants I've mentioned, great thoughts have powerfully influenced many who considered themselves intellectually ordinary. Dwight Moody, for example, had very little formal education, but his life was consumed with a thought expressed by an evangelist he met in Dublin: "The world has yet to see what God will do with and for and through and in and by the man who is fully consecrated to him."[2] Moody wanted to be that man, and because that great thought was deeply rooted in his heart, Christian history has been (and continues to be) profoundly affected by his ministry.

The truth is that a mind flourishing with the deep truths of God is a powerful tool in his hands. Conversely, it simply isn't possible to have a mind filled with flawed, pessimistic, cynical thinking and live an influential, fruitful life for the kingdom of God. If you want your life to dramatically change—to get out of a rut of destructive emotions or bad habits—it all begins with what goes into your mind.

God Commands Great Thinking

Paul's letter to the church at Philippi emphasizes the importance of great thoughts. Throughout the course of the letter, he urges the Philippians to think of themselves as citizens of heaven, to be joyful, to have a mind of humility, not to have a complaining attitude, not to be intimidated by their adversaries, and so on.

Chapter 4 especially addresses a believer's thought life. Paul helps a couple of church members resolve a conflict and re-

minds the fellowship to rejoice in everything. He acknowledges that there will be difficulties in life accompanied by
anxiety and fear, but he tells them to respond by getting rid
of anxiety and turning to thankful prayer. The result will be
the kind of peace that transcends all understanding or human
knowledge.

Having dealt with the negative thoughts surrounding difficulties in life, Paul then turns to a more positive, proactive
approach: "Whatever is true, whatever is honorable, whatever
is right, whatever is pure, whatever is lovely, whatever is of
good repute, if there is any excellence and if anything worthy
of praise, dwell on these things" (Phil. 4:8 NASB).

In doing a word study on *dwell*, I found that the Greek word
logizomai (translated "dwell" in Phil. 4:8) is not a casual word.
It means "to deduce, to reason, to calculate, to ponder, to deliberate, to subject to protracted analysis or thought." It implies
thinking about a matter long enough to take into account its
character and realize its implications for your life. Paul is telling
believers that whatever is characterized by these godly qualities
is worthy of a lot of active meditation. In other words, he tells
them to think great thoughts.

Let's take a look at each of those words Paul uses in his description of great thoughts:

- *True*—think about things that are objectively true, things
  that conform to reality. Before you put something in your
  mind, ask yourself: Is this true?
- *Honorable*—this word also means "grave" or "worthy of
  respect." It refers to those things that reflect the serious
  purposes of a believer's life. Before that movie, commercial,
  or conversation goes into your mind, ask yourself: Does
  this honor God and reflect his purposes for me?
- *Right*—the word implies justice and righteousness. In the
  New Testament, it's used to refer to the character and
  actions of the Father and of Jesus. It is a picture of duty.
  Before you spend time thinking about something, ask
  yourself: Is this right or wrong?

- *Pure*—it comes from the same root word as *holy* and means to be pure from defilement of immorality. It carries the idea of internal integrity. Ask yourself: Am I thinking on things that are pure and holy?
- *Lovely*—this is my favorite word in the list. It means attractive, winsome, or beautiful. It pictures things that call forth a response of love and warmth from within us. Ask yourself: Is my mind filled with beauty?
- *Of good repute*—the general sense of the word is "admirable," but its literal meaning is "fair speaking." In other words, are these thoughts fit for God's hearing?
- *Anything of excellence and worthy of praise*—these last two thoughts are a summary category for anything that has moral excellence, motivates us to godly behavior, or encourages others to walk with God.

Paul urges his readers to practice these things as they have seen them in him, and the God of peace—that transcendent, beyond-understanding peace—will be with them.

What is Paul saying? Get your thoughts right and the emotions, behaviors, and consequences of peace will follow. A spiritually trained mind will align everything else to such a degree that emotional issues will begin to be resolved and behavior will begin to fall into place.

The Bible is very clear about this dynamic in other places as well. Romans 8:6 says that a mind set on the things of the flesh will bring forth death, but a mind set on the Spirit brings forth life and peace. Colossians 3:2 says, "Set your mind on the things above, not on the things that are on earth" (NASB). And Peter tells his readers to prepare their minds for action (1 Peter 1:13). We are to get in the habit of thinking the right thoughts.

You Are What You Think

To express our thought life in terms of a *habit* seems unspiritual to a lot of people, but much of our thinking is undeniably habitual. In fact, most of our behavior is made up of habits, including many we aren't even aware of. Most of us go to bed at a certain time each night. We get up in the morning at a regular time; we brush our teeth a couple of times a day; we grab a cup of coffee at a predictable hour; we get in a car and drive to work, usually the same route every day. No one tells us to do all of these things. We don't even have to remind ourselves of most of them because they're habitual.

It's easy to see the application of this truth physically. If we spend our lives eating donuts and candy bars, drinking several cups of coffee and several cans of soft drinks a day, and never getting much exercise, we can predict a certain level of health down the road. What we put into our bodies is going to determine the quality of life our bodies have.

Paul is simply saying that the mind works the same way. There's a certain kind of thinking that ought to become habitual for us because it will lead to godliness and peace. The presence of God attends to such thoughts. As with our bodies, we may not see the results of our nutritional plan right away, but we will see it over time. Everyone, whether in the flesh or the Spirit, reaps what he sows. John Stott, in his commentary on Galatians, put it this way: "Sow a thought, reap an action. Sow an action, reap a habit. Sow a habit, reap a character. Sow a character, reap a destiny."[3] Eventually, we will be the product of our thinking.

What's Your Mental Diet?

For many people, the practice of meditating on Scripture and spiritual insights seems difficult. I've heard faithful believers tell me they don't have the discipline or the concentration to memorize verses or focus on God's truth for long periods of time without getting distracted. But everyone knows how to do this. Most of us do it when we're anxious and worried; we can concentrate on problems and fears for hours at a time, picking apart every detail and obsessing about every contingency. Thinking great thoughts means taking that incredible ability to focus on negatives and using it for more positive and truthful purposes.

Instead of obsessing about the quandaries you're stuck in—or
might possibly be stuck in if every variable turns out for the worst,
as you expect—try filling your mind with truth instead.

What do you think about when you drive? What do you listen
to at home? When the remote control is in your hand, what
channels do you turn on and allow to flow into your mind? If
you feed your mind on a diet of mental junk food, your spiritual health will reflect it. If, however, you feed your mind on
a diet of eternal truths, the character of God, the promises he
has given, his track record with his people, and everything
else that is true, honorable, right, pure, lovely, of good repute,
excellent, and worthy of praise, your spiritual health will, over
time, prove stronger and more consistent and lasting than you
ever thought possible.

We are people who have been called to ultimate transformation. Romans 12:2 tells us not to be conformed to this world but
to be transformed by the renewing of our mind, with the result
that we will prove and experience the will of God. Though we
live in a fallen world and fight in a daily battle, God's will for
us is good and pleasing. According to Scripture, we can only
experience it through a renewed mind. And we can only experience a renewed mind by filling it with great thoughts.

Sources of Great Thoughts

How do we begin to think great thoughts? In a world that
overwhelms us with endless varieties of philosophies and values,
where do we learn the thoughts of God?

Start with Scripture. For me, John 8:32 is key: "You will know
the truth, and the truth will set you free." It's a familiar verse,
but I don't think we always realize how broad its promise is. If
I want to be free of anxiety, of fear, of the expectations of others, of habits that enslave me, and of negative emotions—and,
positively, if I want to be all God longs for me to be—I've got
to saturate my mind with truth.

Let me emphasize that I'm not simply talking about a Bible-
reading program. A lot of people have a checklist to keep them

moving through the Bible in a daily reading plan—which can be very helpful, by the way—but a reading plan alone is not going to get great thoughts into your mind. Absorbing the Word of God, thinking it over when you lie down and get up, and lingering in the depths of his revelation will cultivate great thoughts. Charles Spurgeon urged his students, "Let us, dear brethren, try to *get saturated with the gospel*. I always find that I can preach best when I can lie a-soak in my text. I like to get a text, and find out its meanings and bearings, and so on; and then, after I have bathed in it, I delight to lie down in it, and let it soak into me."[4] That's how God wants to fill your heart and mind with the truth that is in Scripture. If you will soak in that truth and drink deeply from it, you are going to be free.

The alternative, of course, is to believe a lie. If we're like sponges, absorbing any billboard, magazine, movie, song, book, and so on, we'll naturally take in a lot of deception along the way. That may sound like an overreaction to media influences, but the course of many lives has been influenced by such casual absorption. Thinking great thoughts is a deliberate, intentional process of informing our mind with truth.

Think again about how deliberate we can be when it comes to our physical nutrition. Thirty years ago, if you pulled a can of vegetables off the shelf, it listed one ingredient: the vegetable itself. Today you'll find a breakdown of protein, carbohydrates, and fat, as well as how much fiber and vitamin content is in there. Fast food restaurants have charts telling us exactly what's in the food we're eating. Those labels and charts are there in large part because of popular demand. Many people today are extremely fastidious about counting calories and nutritional milligrams. We can be downright obsessed with our intake.

It's amazing to me that our culture can be so smart and deliberate about physical nutrition and so mindless about the spiritual, intellectual, and emotional content of the ideas we consume. We're casual about what goes into our minds and then end up in therapy desperately trying to change what's in there. I'm convinced that if we took half the care to guard our minds that we do to guard our bodies, in about five years we would be amazed at the transformation that has taken place in our heart and relationships.

Dwell on great truths. In addition to Scripture, many people have learned valuable truth from their experiences in life. One example is a famous quote by Jim Elliot, one of the five missionaries who died at the hands of the Aucas of Ecuador in the 1950s: "He is no fool who gives what he cannot keep in order to gain what he cannot lose." That's a truth I don't want to forget. I want to meditate on it and let it soak into my mind and become a part of me. As I live in a materialistic society and watch all the advertisements that tell me I'm missing something, that I don't look right, that I'd be happy if only I had this car or that mouthwash, I need a constant mental reminder that I'm living for eternal values. Great thoughts like that of Jim Elliot serve as that reminder.

> "He is no fool who gives what he cannot keep
> to gain what he cannot lose."
>
> —*Jim Elliot*

Another example is a well-known prayer of St. Francis of Assisi:

> Lord, make me an instrument of your peace.
> Where there is hatred, let me sow love;
> where there is injury, pardon;
> where there is doubt, faith;
> where there is despair, hope;
> where there is darkness, light;
> and where there is sadness, joy. . . .

And it goes on with a treasure of inspiring thoughts. My mind is inevitably going to be filled with something; why not let it be filled with a prayer like that instead of a song on MTV, a half-hour of sports talk, the last commercial I saw, or the plot of tonight's sitcom?

Take time to notice beauty. Another source of great thoughts is beauty. When I lived in Santa Cruz, I could see the ocean from my house. In seven minutes, I could be in the Santa Cruz mountains and see the tallest trees in the world. When life got really busy, I could find a place to get away and sense the grandeur of creation. Sometimes on Sunday morning, I'd feel like my sermon preparation and notes were ready to preach but my heart wasn't. So I would get a cup of coffee, sit overlooking the bay, watch the waves crash, and just stare. I would think of how I could only see a little part of a big ocean, which is only one ocean on this little planet, which is part of a small solar system in one galaxy, which is only one small galaxy among billions. And here I am, a tiny little guy uptight about what people might think about my sermon.

"The heavens declare the glory of God" (Ps. 19:1). It's impossible to dwell on the beauty of creation and continue to be self-absorbed. My times of soaking in the grandeur reminded me how small my focus had gotten and how big my God is. It restored great thoughts to a mind that had become overwhelmed with a lot of trivial ones.

Once I've spent some time considering the enormity and goodness of God, I find it encouraging to focus specifically on some of his promises. Great thoughts about the Promiser always lead to great thoughts about the promises. Remember, for example, that the one who said all power in heaven and earth had been given to him is the one who said he goes with us until the end of the age (Matt. 28:18–20). When you don't feel like going to work because of what you'll face there, remember his words: "I am with you always." When you need to confront one of your kids and you know there will be a big blow-up, remember: "I am with you always." When you've made some really bad decisions and now there isn't enough money at the end of the month, remember: "I am with you always."

Those words mean a lot any time, but when you've meditated often on the grandeur of the one who spoke them, they are energizing and inspiring. They have the power to pull you out of an emotional pit. So do Jesus's sweeping promises about prayer or his blanket assurances about the future welfare of his people. A high view of God elevates his words in your mind and builds in you the faith to believe them.

A high view of God elevates his words in your mind and builds in you the faith to believe them.

Meditate on spiritual insights. Finally, great thoughts can come from personal insights God has given you in specific situations in your life. The Holy Spirit has a way of working life lessons into your heart, and they become more and more a part of you as you meditate on them and let them sink in. One of mine, for example, was the realization that I'm not the only person in the world who is desperately insecure. Everyone is. That was a lightbulb that came on in my mind long ago, and it has taken a lot of pressure off ever since. I stopped worrying about positioning myself in a meeting so everyone would think well of me or of dressing the right way and saying the right things to impress the right people. Once I understood that everyone is insecure, it gave me the freedom to acknowledge my hang-ups, assume others have similar hang-ups, and just be authentic with people. I could look for my security in Christ rather than in the opinions of others. That's an insight I want to keep and dwell on so it becomes more and more a part of who I am.

Another insight I keep coming back to is that God loves me at this moment as much as he ever has and as much as he ever will. My performance isn't going to change that. It is true on good days and on bad days. There are blessings that will come with obedience, of course, and consequences that will come with disobedience, but God's love doesn't change. I'm as loved right now as I ever will be, and nothing will ever diminish that love.

I'll share one more insight that has changed my life: comparison is at the core of carnality. That comes straight out of 2 Corinthians 10:12, so there's nothing groundbreaking there. But when I internalized that truth, it made a huge difference in my life. I realized that when I compare my gifts with someone else's, there are only two places to go: inferiority or superiority. I either become envious or arrogant. It's the same when I compare personalities, success, possessions, relationships, or anything else. There's no spiritual benefit to doing that, and it comes out of a carnal, self-centered heart. This universal human tendency to compare can result in all kinds of emotional struggles. What's the solution? To think about the truth: we are accepted in Christ by his blood; we're the object of his affection; we are so precious to him that he gathers our tears in a bottle (Ps. 56:8 NASB), and he went to the cross while we were still sinners. We are accepted in the Beloved, and the life we now live is a response of gratitude, not a labor of guilt or a desperate attempt to impress. The Christian life flows out of a whole different way of thinking.

Those are great thoughts. Those are the kinds of thoughts that lead to a sense of security that allows people of faith to dream great dreams and take great risks. Great thoughts like that relieve the knots in your stomach when you go to a meeting, and they allow you to give your teenager what she needs instead of what she wants, even if peace in the home suffers for a moment. When we meditate on the truths of the gospel, we eventually internalize them. And when they become internalized, they are life-changing.

I saw amazing proof of this principle in college when a guy named George Dzundra began coming to a Thursday night Bible study I attended. George wasn't very cool. He was one of those socially awkward people that every group seems to have. He spoke with a lisp, he was already balding, he had zero self-esteem, and he was terribly insecure. Being around him was okay on Thursday nights in a Christian group where everyone's supposed to be accepted. But when I hung out with guys on the basketball team, I was embarrassed to be seen with him. If he came up to me and started talking, I'd get out of the conversation as quickly as I could.

At some point during college, someone taught George the power of thinking great thoughts. He began to memorize Scripture, and he didn't do it halfway. I didn't see him for a few months, and when I ran into him again, his pocket was full of index cards with memory verses on them. He had memorized all of James and the Gospels of John and Matthew, as well as a couple of Paul's letters. He filled his mind with the promises of God and had begun dwelling on his identity in Christ rather than his own insecurities. Having the Word of God so deeply in his mind had completely changed him. He was rooted in the knowledge that God loved him, and it showed. He was much more confident and mature. He radiated God's Spirit.

Before long, guys who normally wouldn't even associate with someone like George began coming to him for advice. He listened to their problems and shared God's wisdom with them. I found myself asking if he and I could hang out together, and spending time with him taught me a lot about what God had been doing in his life. George was the most amazing transformation I had ever seen in such a short period of time.

I shared that story without using George's last name when I was teaching a few years ago. Not long afterward, I received an email from George's wife asking if I could possibly be the same Chip Ingram who had attended West Liberty State College in West Virginia—and if the George I was talking about could possibly be her husband. Turns out he had gone to seminary and become a pastor after college. I wrote back and told her how deeply her husband had impacted me. He made a lasting impression on how the power of renewing the mind with great thoughts can change the course of a person's life.

Key Areas for Cultivating Great Thoughts

Learning to think great thoughts is a constant, lifelong process—and, for a lot of people, it is a random process. I've found the following seven areas to be the most foundational and the most critical for bringing our minds into alignment with truth.

1. *Think great thoughts about God.* A good passage to start with is Romans 11:33–36:

> Oh, the depth of the riches of the wisdom and knowl-
>   edge of God!
>   How unsearchable his judgments,
>   and his paths beyond tracing out!
> "Who has known the mind of the Lord?
>   Or who has been his counselor?"
> "Who has ever given to God,
>   that God should repay him?"
> For from him and through him and to him are all things.
>   To him be the glory forever! Amen.

Spend some time trying to wrap your mind around all the implications of that passage, and you'll end up with a rather high view of your Creator.

2. *Think great thoughts about yourself.* It seems unspiritual to think about yourself at all, doesn't it? But unless you understand something about yourself, you can't really understand God's love for you. You need to understand just how much you need his mercy, and you need to understand just how much of it he has given. Let Zephaniah 3:17 stretch your mind:

> The LORD your God is with you,
>   he is mighty to save.
> He will take great delight in you,
>   he will quiet you with his love,
>   he will rejoice over you with singing.

What if you woke up each morning thinking about the God of the universe singing a song of rejoicing over you? What if you thought about yourself as the object of the eternal God's love, regardless of whether you have your act together today? Would that change your life? Do you think your self-perception would remain *good*? Or would it improve drastically to *great*?

3. *Think great thoughts about others.* How does God look at people? According to 1 Samuel 16:7, "The LORD does not look at the things man looks at. Man looks at the outward appearance, but the LORD looks at the heart." What do you think would happen to your relationships if you began to see people as God sees them? Most people try to see into the heart but still get caught up in external appearance, status, success, or possessions. God sees who we really are inside. If you looked for the beauty of each person's heart and began forming relationships on that basis alone, you'd end up with more friends than most people can imagine. You would also find yourself in a position to minister God's love in ways you never have before.

4. *Think great thoughts about life.* After Jesus asked his disciples who they thought he was, and Peter got it right by identifying him as the Christ, Jesus told them how he would suffer. Then he described his perspective on life: "If anyone would come after me, he must deny himself and take up his cross daily and follow me. For whoever wants to save his life will lose it, but whoever loses his life for me will save it. What good is it for a man to gain the whole world, and yet lose or forfeit his very self?" (Luke 9:23–25).

Life isn't about acquiring, accumulating, impressing, or exploiting. It's about discovering God's agenda, taking up your cross, and following Jesus. You lose your life in the process, but you gain his life. That's a great thought, and it's radically different than anything the world teaches. When that great thought sinks in, you begin to live with an entirely new perspective.

5. *Think great thoughts about the future.* Can you imagine living life without fear and anxiety, without worry about what tomorrow will bring and stress about how to make everything work out? You can live that way if you believe what God has promised in Jeremiah 29:11: "'I know the plans I have for you,' declares the LORD, 'plans to prosper

you and not to harm you, plans to give you hope and a future.'" God is sovereign, and he has a plan not only for the universe but also for you personally. You can save all the energy most people expend thinking about terrorism, the economy, how your kids will turn out, and so forth and instead invest that energy in something more productive. Why? Because you have a promise that God is in control and he has your welfare in mind. That doesn't mean your life will be problem-free, but it does mean you don't have to worry about whether those problems will thwart God's purposes for you. Worry and anxiety are not great thoughts; faith in God's promise is.

6. *Think great thoughts about the past.* For a lot of people, their past has crippled their future. They have a hard time letting their mistakes go. Paul's great thought on that subject was this: "Forgetting what lies behind and reaching forward to what lies ahead, I press on toward the goal for the prize of the upward call of God in Christ Jesus" (Phil. 3:13–14 NASB). The psalmist says that our sins are removed from us as far as the east is from the west (Ps. 103:12). That's how God thinks about our past, and we're supposed to do the same.

7. *Think great thoughts about challenges.* We let adversity get us down, turn us into a victim, make us angry at God, or we live with nagging regrets. We allow ourselves to be eaten up about the raw deal we've been handed—the dad who left when we were young, the bad investment that left us with no financial security, and so on. We have no shortage of unhealthy ways to address the challenges of our lives.

Meanwhile, James 1:2–4 tells us this: "Consider it all joy, my brethren, when you encounter various trials, knowing that the testing of your faith produces endurance. And let endurance have its perfect result, so that you may be perfect and complete, lacking in nothing" (NASB). That's a radically different way to think, but if that thought drives us when we face a trial, our emotions, behaviors, and consequences will look much different than if our minds follow their natural, unhealthy course. In these and all other areas, when our minds are filled with great thoughts, our lives eventually bear great fruit.

Some Practical Tips to Get You Started

As we've discussed, a transformed thought life doesn't just happen. It's a matter of practice and developing habits. There are very practical steps you can take to think great thoughts. In fact, the very first psalm gives us a picture of how to take those steps.

> How blessed is the man who does not walk in the coun-
>   sel of the wicked,
>   Nor stand in the path of sinners,
>   Nor sit in the seat of scoffers!
> But his delight is in the law of the LORD,
>   And in His law he meditates day and night.
> He will be like a tree firmly planted by streams of water,
>   Which yields its fruit in its season
>   And its leaf does not wither;
>   And in whatever he does, he prospers.
>
> The wicked are not so,
>   But they are like chaff which the wind drives away.
> Therefore the wicked will not stand in the judgment,
>   Nor sinners in the assembly of the righteous.
> For the LORD knows the way of the righteous,
>   But the way of the wicked will perish.
>
> Psalm 1:1–6 NASB

How blessed is the person who does not fall in line with people going in the wrong direction, who does not put himself or herself in a position of absorbing the same lies, who has no need to look like, act like, and have the same things as those who do not know God. Notice the contrast: his or her delight is in the law of the Lord. He or she loves truth and meditates on it all the time. What's the result? "He will be like a tree firmly planted by streams of water, which yields its fruit in its season." It's a picture of prosperity, and it's brought about by thinking great thoughts.

I'll close with a few suggestions for how to do this. They may seem kind of obvious, and I'm sure you can come up with many more that fit your personality and lifestyle just as well, but these will help you get started.

- *Memorize and meditate on Scripture.* This isn't an "ought to" that will make you feel incredibly guilty if you don't. It should be a "want to" that you can have fun with. Write down some verses on index cards, stick them in your pocket, and read them over whenever you have a little down time waiting in line or between meetings. Take a look at them before you go to bed and when you wake up in the morning—make them the first and last thing you put in your mind each day.

- *Use your drive time.* Do you really need to hear the latest sports talk or meaningless music? Listen to tapes of the Bible, or let your mind enjoy some silence while you ponder deep truths.

- *Listen to great music.* There's a connection between music and our emotions that I don't really understand, but the scriptural basis for making music is undeniable. The command to sing occurs surprisingly often, and David's music was able to soothe Saul's restless spirit. Refreshing and uplifting music can set the course your mind will follow.

- *Take walks in nature.* Go somewhere beautiful, even if it's in your own backyard. Wherever you live, you can find some aspect of nature to enjoy as you contemplate the marvels of creation.

- *Personalize scriptural truth and promises.* Write down some passages that address your specific issues, even writing your name in place of whatever pronouns the passage uses. Make it personal and applicable to your individual struggles and needs. I've got some of these on cards that I've carried with me for years.

When the truth resonates with your heart, you'll notice your emotions changing and you'll find yourself motivated to do things that surprise you. Thinking great thoughts will be just the first step in a radically changed life. Set your mind on the things above, dwell on whatever is true and honorable and right. And the God of peace will be with you.

Action Steps

1. One day this week, find a spot where you can focus on creation. Consider the wisdom that God put into all the details of this world. Think about the power that created it out of nothing. Look up into the sky and try to wrap your mind around the distance between you and the farthest galaxy. Let the magnificence of the universe remind you of the awesome nature of God and the small (by comparison) and temporary nature of your problems.

2. As much as possible, isolate yourself from media for forty-eight hours this week. Substitute time you would normally spend reading the newspaper, watching TV, reading a magazine, and so on with listening to praise music. Let nothing but praise and worship enter your ears. At the end of your forty-eight-hour media fast, try to notice whether your perspective and attitude have changed at all.

3. Memorize Philippians 4:8, "Finally, brethren, whatever is true, whatever is honorable, whatever is right, whatever is pure, whatever is lovely, whatever is of good repute, if there is any excellence and if anything worthy of praise, dwell on these things" (NASB).

Questions for Reflection and Discussion

1. What is your biggest struggle in your thought life? What are you currently doing to nourish that negative thought pattern? What are you currently doing to nourish a positive substitute for it?
2. Why do you think it's easier for most people to be absorbed in negative thoughts than positive ones?
3. How do you think your life would change if you spent more time thinking about how much God loves, protects, and provides for you than about the problems you're facing right now? What practical steps can you take to find out?

2

Read Great Books

Many years ago when I was in Hong Kong, I met a missionary who had a razor-sharp mind and a tender heart. I knew I wanted to learn from him. I entered his study in one of the city's enormous high-rises. It was a huge room filled with books, and against one wall were rows and rows of paperbacks.

"I make it a matter of discipline to read one Christian paperback a day," he told me.

"You mean a week?" I asked.

"No, a day."

I was in awe. Then this speed reader got up, walked over to the wall of paperbacks, pulled out a thin book, and handed it to me.

"Have you ever seen this?" he asked.

I shook my head.

"Well, you've got about a week before you leave Hong Kong. Why don't you read it and give it back to me before you leave?"

I reached out and took the book—*The Knowledge of the Holy*, by A. W. Tozer—and opened to the first page. "What comes into our minds when we think about God is the most important

thing about us," it began. What a way to start a book, I thought.
It went on: "For this reason, the gravest question before the
Church is always God Himself, and the most portentous fact
about any man is not what he at a given time may say or do,
but what he in his deep heart conceives God to be like."[1]

That stunned me, and I was zealous to get deeper into it. I
devoured each of the short chapters in that book—I was especially impacted by the chapter on the goodness of God, which
radically changed how I think about him—and then I read
each chapter again. When it came time to return the book, the
missionary decided to let me keep it. I carried that copy in my
briefcase for twenty-six years until my wife gave me an updated
edition for my birthday one year. Now I carry the new one.

The reason I've kept it in my briefcase is because I keep
reading it over and over. It has the most profound thoughts
about God that I've ever read. I grew up with a view of God as
a cosmic policeman who had a club he was waiting to use on
me. When I read that God takes holy pleasure in the happiness
of his people, that he has a good plan, and that I'm the object
of his affection, it was all so foreign to me that I had to reread
it several times for it to begin to sink in.

"The whole outlook of mankind might be changed if we could
all believe that we dwell under a friendly sky," Tozer writes, "and
that the God of heaven, though exalted in power and majesty,
is eager to be friends with us."[2] Now when I bow my head to
pray, I think of a God who loves to hear my heart. Nothing is
too big or too small. He's eager to be my friend and yours.

Rereading *The Knowledge of the Holy* as often as I do keeps
me focused on God. It's easy for me, as it is for all of us, to turn
inward and start thinking life is all about myself. This book
reminds me that life does not ultimately revolve around my
dreams, my agenda, my fulfillment, my significance and security, my marriage and kids, my work, and so on. It's ultimately
about God. That singular focus transforms every relationship
and every thought.

I've quoted Tozer here because I want to emphasize just how
profoundly a book can change your perspective. "Read great
books" doesn't sound very exciting or very life-changing, but

it can be. I'll share in this chapter many of the books that have impacted me over the years, but not because I want you to go get the same ones and read them. I want you to catch a vision, to realize that you can sit under the teaching of history's greatest minds and most devoted hearts, and to see how a life can be transformed by the experiences of those who have lived by faith and experienced God's work.

The Greatest Book

God himself appreciates the value of books, as evidenced by the fact that he chose to reveal himself to us in a collection of them. That revelation came in the real experiences of real people, of course, but we would know nothing of God's truth today if inspired people had not taken the time to write it down. The Bible is full of biographies, historical events, God's dealings with his people, praise, poetry, and prophecy. Not only does it come across as essential reading on eternal truths, it even contains commands to read it and provides examples of its power. God has transformed people's lives through the written word for centuries.

Deuteronomy 6:6–9 says it clearly: "These commandments that I give you today are to be upon your hearts. Impress them on your children. Talk about them when you sit at home and when you walk along the road, when you lie down and when you get up. Tie them as symbols on your hands and bind them on your foreheads. Write them on the doorframes of your houses and on your gates." The words of sacred Hebrew books were to become the focus of mentoring relationships, the topic of daily conversations, and the object of serious study. Why? Because there's power in the written word.

That's one of the reasons each king of Israel was required by God's law to write every word of the law on a scroll when he first took the throne (Deut. 17:18). God did not want his people to be ruled by a man who had not scrutinized his written Word. Most kings did not fulfill this command, but God's purpose in it is clear. Those who read truth are more likely to live it out.

Joshua read every word of God's law out loud to the entire assembly of Israel (Josh. 8:34–35). King Josiah read the same words to Judah, and the people were moved to dedicate themselves to heeding them (2 Chron. 34:29–33). Daniel read Jeremiah's prophecy about the length of Israel's captivity, and it prompted him to plead with God in prayer and fasting (Dan. 9:2–3). In Nehemiah, the priests read God's Word to the people, and it caused them to weep in confession and repentance (Neh. 8:8–9; 9:3). Peter urged Christians to read the letters of Paul (2 Peter 3:15–16). All of these examples teach us how important it is to learn from those who have experienced God's truth in the past.

Great Books Broaden Your World

I was a young Christian when I started reading biographies. The first one I read was *Daws: The Story of Dawson Trotman, Founder of the Navigators*, by Betty Lee Skinner.[3] Trotman was a young unbeliever who had a crush on a cute girl, and together they went to a youth meeting at her church where the group was having a memory verse contest. Being a competitive guy, he determined to win the contest for memorizing the most verses. He went back the next week, said all ten perfectly, and was shocked to find out that none of the Christian kids had memorized all of them.

Not long after, Trotman had an experience that startled him. He was walking along the street when the words, "For all have sinned and fall short of the glory of God" came to him. That surprised him—until he remembered that he had memorized that verse (Rom. 3:23). A little further down the street, he was struck by another verse: "The wages of sin is death, but the free gift of God is eternal life in Christ Jesus our Lord" (Rom. 6:23 NASB). And then a little further: "God demonstrates His own love toward us, in that while we were yet sinners, Christ died for us" (Rom. 5:8 NASB). Trotman realized the Spirit of God was bringing these verses to mind.

The last verse that popped into his head that day changed him forever: "Behold, I stand at the door, and knock: if any man hear my voice, and open the door, I will come in to him, and will sup with him, and he with me" (Rev. 3:20 KJV). And it was followed up by a personal message: "Dawson, you can have eternal life."

Right there on the street, this near dropout trusted Jesus, and from that point on his biography is a story of a man with passion and focus who learns to pray for every county in California, then every state in the U.S., then every country of the world. He began a powerful ministry that focused on Scripture memory and personal discipleship.

At the time I read *Daws*, the Navigators were all over the world on every major college campus and in the military. I learned from that biography that an ordinary guy with a high school education can, with God's Spirit working through him, change the world. That removed any pressure to become a brilliant scholar, to have a lot of money, or to be extremely popular and influential. Someone with a passion for Christ who believes God's Word is true can impact millions of people for God's glory.

A few months later, I picked up a copy of *Uncle Cam*, the life story of Cameron Townsend, the man who founded Wycliffe Bible Translators.[4] Townsend went to Guatemala in 1917 to sell Spanish Bibles among the Cakchiquel people. He soon discovered that the majority of those he met did not understand Spanish and there was no written form of their own language. When Cakchiquel-speaking men expressed their concern and surprise that God did not speak their language, Townsend realized that unless people hear God's Word in their own language—not just a language they can speak, but the language of their heart—they could never be reached with the gospel.

God had taken another ordinary man and given him a passion to get the Bible translated into every known language in the world. Today, Wycliffe translators lead the field in the study of linguistics and have had a part in translating the New Testament into over 600 minority and indigenous languages with Wycliffe personnel currently working in Bible translation, literacy, and/or preparatory linguistic work in over 1,300 languages.[5]

The third book I read around that time was *Hudson Taylor's Spiritual Secret*.[6] Taylor was a missionary to China in the late 1800s, and his life is filled with life-changing lessons about faith, God's heart for the lost, and the courage to be innovative in fulfilling the Great Commission. Taylor founded the China Inland Mission, which still exists today as the Overseas Missionary Fellowship. He went against mainstream missionary practices, adopted Chinese clothes and customs, and reached parts of the country no Christian had ever reached. His passion was contagious, and his complete dependence on God was inspiring. It opened my eyes to the possibility of a deeper life with Jesus.

I learned from these three books that God uses ordinary people to do extraordinary things. I was in my early twenties, and I realized that I didn't have to be the most spiritual and most gifted guy in the world. God began to change my life through these biographies, and not only did I learn from the stories of these very real people, I began to read Scripture through the same lens. I began to notice that the Bible doesn't cover up the weaknesses and failures of God's greatest heroes and that God has always used ordinary people to do extraordinary things.

Another book I read during this time of my life was a short paperback exposition of Romans 12 by Jay Adams of Westminster Seminary.[7] I had never seen or heard an "exposition." I had only heard teachers who used verses from all over Scripture, which had taught me a lot. But in this book on Romans 12 the author gives an overview of the first eleven chapters, and then he explains verse by verse what chapter 12 means and how it fits with the rest of Paul's letter. He opens the Bible in a way that made me want to learn every chapter of the Bible the same way.

So I started getting up early in the morning and going through a chapter of the Bible each day, writing and rewriting them so I could explain them in plain English the way Adams had done in his book. I later heard someone from Dallas Seminary teach the same way out of 1 John. I knew nothing about seminaries at that time, but I knew I wanted to learn how to do that kind of study. The thought that an ordinary person like me could open up the Bible, study a chapter, and understand what it meant to the original audience, what it means to me, and how to respond to it, began a lifelong journey.

Great Books Sharpen Your Mind

The next era of books that changed my life came when I was involved in college ministry and had been a coach and a school teacher for a while. I realized that if I wanted to be a college coach, I had to go to graduate school. I enrolled at West Virginia University.

I had been a Christian for about five years at this point, and I knew the reality of a life of faith. God had changed my life, and I had seen him change others too. But whenever I was around these intellectual professors and graduate students who challenged my beliefs and faith, I began to feel like they were really big and I was really small—or, even worse, that they were really smart and I was really dumb. I had a nagging question of whether I needed to throw my brains in the trash in order to be a follower of Christ. And I even began to ask myself: Can I really believe this?

In the midst of that struggle, I met a Christian premed student who introduced me to the books of Francis Schaeffer. Schaeffer had been a pastor in the United States who moved to Switzerland and established L'Abri Fellowship, a place where intellectuals came from all over the world and asked honest questions about faith. Three of his books that are the foundation for all of his writing are *Escape from Reason*, *The God Who Is There*, and *He Is There and He Is Not Silent*.[8] For those who like to ask the big philosophical questions about life and faith, these are landmark books.

I began a journey in which those three books became as familiar as the back of my hand. I found a Christian professor, explained that I was searching for an intellectual apologetic for my faith, and asked if I could write my thesis on the philosophical basis for teaching ethics in sports. I analyzed Schaeffer's books, wrote my thesis, and defended it the day before Theresa and I got married.

The defense lasted three and a half hours. I sat before four professors whose job it was to take shots at my thesis and try to tear holes in it. I learned during that time that the deeper you dig into Christianity and understand its logic, the archaeology that supports it, and the philosophical basis for believing, the more you feel like you're on solid ground with your faith. As these professors—one in particular—tried to prove that truth is relative, I became increasingly secure in my argument. The discussion ended when one professor said to another, "Andy, give it up. He's backing you into a corner, and you're never going to win this one. I don't believe the Bible either, but we aren't going to win the argument that there's no such thing as absolute truth. We all know it. He's backed us into a corner and there's no logical way out."

I walked out of that defense realizing that God has revealed his truth and wisdom to certain people over the course of time—Schaeffer was the one I was most grateful for at that moment—and God's truth is available to anyone who seeks it. That session shaped my life and gave me a new confidence in the Bible. But I also realized you can't get that confidence from someone else. You can learn from them, but convictions are born out of self-study when the Spirit of God takes truth and makes it real in your heart.

After depending so heavily on Francis Schaeffer for my thesis, I didn't really want to read any more of his books for a while. But I found out about *True Spirituality*,[9] a book that's less philosophical than his others and explains how the spiritual life works. For someone like me, who didn't grow up reading the Bible or going to church very often, it helped me fit everything together. I had been trying to do what God wanted me to do, but I just couldn't figure out how it was all supposed to work. When I was disciplined, I'd be a self-righteous jerk, and when I wasn't disciplined, I was overwhelmed with guilt. Being a Christian was so exciting and relational at first, but then as I learned more of what you're supposed to do as a Christian—and *not* supposed to do—it started to feel like an overwhelming burden.

God used Schaeffer's *True Spirituality* to bring me back to the core of what it means to walk with God. It reminded me that the Christian life is a relationship. It's all about being united with Christ, both in his death and in his resurrection. Life is no longer about simply going to church or being moral and nice; it's a relationship that you live out in a spirit of gratitude. The Word of God empowered by the Spirit of God in the community of God's people transforms you little by little as you get to know him. Schaeffer's systematic and logical focus on how to grasp my identity in Christ was totally liberating for me.

I also received an important warning from that book about spiritual pride. Every Christian I've ever known—including myself—who has broken through to significant levels of being used by God goes through a phase of being satisfied with their growth, discipline, prayer, generosity, or love. Then they begin to look down on everyone else as people who just need to get with the program. I was in the process of becoming an obnoxious jerk who had memorized a lot of verses and read a lot of books, and I started thinking I knew more than everyone else. That kind of pride is no fun to be around.

Schaeffer taught me that the true test of spiritual maturity is not knowledge but love for God and love for others. The test of love for God is whether at any given moment you can say "thank you" for what's happening in your life, and the test of love for others is whether you are free from envy. I failed both of those tests, and it sent me on a journey.

Great Books Inflame Your Heart

During that journey, I was impacted by three books in particular: *Power Through Prayer,* by E. M. Bounds; *Humility: The Beauty of Holiness,* by Andrew Murray; and *The Calvary Road,* by Roy Hession.[10]

My desire to read about prayer was stirred by my relationship with my wife, Theresa. When she and I were dating, I had always noticed that she had a particularly deep relationship with God. She didn't come to Christ the same way I did and didn't have all the same categories and formulas that I was developing. But whenever we prayed together, I always left feeling like he had been there. She talked with him in a very familiar tone: "Lord, you know we just talked about this yesterday," or "God, I know you wouldn't do that—that's just not like you." There was a depth of intimacy that, honestly, was foreign to me. I had tons of knowledge about God but a rather formal relationship with him.

One book that shaped Theresa early in her Christian life was *What Happens When Women Pray*, by Evelyn Christenson.[11] She learned to pray at a level I was unfamiliar with. When I read E. M. Bounds's powerful little book, it helped me grow deeper in my prayer life. I'll never forget some of its very convicting explanations of God's purposes for prayer.

Bounds's basic premise was this: "What the church needs today is not more machinery or better, not new organizations or more and novel methods, but men whom the Holy Ghost can use—men of prayer, men mighty in prayer."[12]

I'm the kind of personality who does things in extreme, so I decided to get up an hour early every morning and pray for an hour, then have my quiet time, and then go to work. Nine months later, I ended up in the hospital because I wasn't getting enough sleep. My zeal for God and my desire to grow were admirable, but my youthful ignorance of how to take care of my body was not. Obviously, I'm not recommending an unbalanced or unhealthy lifestyle, but I did learn a couple of things: (1) I learned to pray; and (2) I learned that the most accurate barometer of my humility and sense of dependency is not what I think about myself or what other people think about me. It's the reality of the actual praying I do.

When we ask God to intervene in our lives or in someone else's life, we're actually admitting our own weakness. We come to God because we know we can't handle whatever situation we're in. We need help with our marriage, our kids, our future, our job, our decisions, or whatever else we seek his help for. On the other hand, when we don't pray very much, we're really saying that even though the Lord created the universe, we think we can handle our problems and guide ourselves through life. It means that we are putting a lot of stock in our own intelligence and resources, quietly claiming our own sufficiency. Genuine prayer acknowledges who God is and our need for him. That's a sign of humility.

Andrew Murray's book on holiness took a different angle. Murray wrote numerous books on the devotional life, but I was drawn to this one in particular. It was hard to read, but I've learned that God's treasures are not mined on the surface. You have to dig down deep and really search for them. *Humility: The Beauty of Holiness* did that, and I couldn't put it down.

The premise of the book is that the beauty of holiness is humility. The Son of God, the Creator of everything that is, left the glory of heaven and the worship of angels to be born on a dirty little planet to a teenager in a smelly stable. He considered others more important than himself. Instead of insisting on what was rightfully due him—worship—he focused on the needs of others, even to the point of death.

Murray told the life story of Jesus through the lens of humility, and it was so attractive that I wanted to give up every prideful motive I'd ever had. The Christian life that seemed so burdensome earlier started to shift. I saw the beauty of wanting to be like Jesus, and all the striving and laboring turned into a joyful pursuit.

Then Roy Hession's book, *The Calvary Road*, taught me that life is about going to the cross. There is no resurrection until there is a crucifixion. Once when I was reading this book, I had to put it down because I got so depressed as I realized how full of myself I was. Jesus said that anyone who wanted to follow him had to deny himself and take up his cross. That's a rare concept in American Christianity today, but genuine discipleship means you go to the cross and you die. Not sort of die, not die to 90 percent of your agenda, but completely die. You say, "Lord, it's not my money, my time, my dreams, my family, my career, . . . it's all yours." You lay it all on the altar, no matter how scary that is, because God is good and generous and will give back whatever he wants you to have. Resurrection power won't come in your life until you become a living sacrifice.

Great Books Develop Your Skills

The next phase of my life was learning how to walk with God as a family. Theresa came to Christ in the aftermath of being abandoned by her first husband. She was alone with two little boys, and when she met Jesus she was beautifully transformed. After we got married and went on a honeymoon for a few days, I came home to a family. I didn't know anything about being a husband, and I knew even less about being a father. So once again, I sought out books by people whom God had taken through difficult family situations.

One of the first great books I read about family life was *The Christian Family*, by Larry Christenson.[13] It wasn't complicated—perfect for a guy like me. In essence it said, "You are the man, this is the woman, and your job is to love her like this." And it spelled out ways to do that. Then it said, "You are the father, and you need to create a family altar and make sure you spend time together with God and his Word." It went on to describe how to discipline children lovingly and firmly. It covered the basics very well, and it was exactly what I needed.

I realized another need soon afterward. Theresa and I both come from backgrounds that make us rather obvious "trophies of grace." Neither of us came to Christ early in our lives, and though our parents cared for us, they couldn't give away what they didn't have: a relationship with Christ. We were relatively new Christians, and it didn't take us long to realize that you can love God with all your heart, love each other with all your heart, and still drive each other absolutely crazy.

Together we read *Communication: Key to Your Marriage*, by H. Norman Wright.[14] I learned one thing from that book that transformed my marriage: talking is not communication. Communication is the meeting of meanings, and I haven't communicated with my wife until she knows what's really on my heart and mind. I also haven't heard her until I understand what's on her heart—not just what she said or did, but what was really behind it. Every week as we went through the book chapter by chapter, we filled in the blanks for each question and talked about our marriage. That probably did more good than anything else.

Marriage, of course, is a lifelong learning process. About fifteen years into ours, we came across another book that made a tremendous difference in our lives. *The Intimacy Factor*, by David and Jan Stoop,[15] had one of those psychological/personality tests that tell you about your thought processes. Theresa and I had already gone through many of those and had some marriage counseling along the way, and I assumed we'd covered it all. I doubted that there was anything new out there that could make a huge difference. Besides, we were doing quite well already.

The book explained that some people are concrete in their thinking and others are abstract or conceptual. We knew that, but we had never learned how to apply it to our marriage. When we realized how this difference was affecting our marriage, we were able to avoid a lot of conflict. For example, Theresa is a concrete thinker; the book calls that "thinking with dots." I, on the other hand, am more abstract; that's called "thinking with dashes." So when Theresa says we're having dinner at 5:30 and I say I'll be there, that's a dot. At 5:35 I'm late, and at 5:40 I've broken my word. All of a sudden, she feels like she's married to a man who has no integrity. That's what's going on in her mind. In my mind, though, 5:30 means any time between about 5:10 and 5:50, and if I'm there at any point in that "dash," I've kept my word.

Recognizing that difference led to a few creative discussions. I came to realize that my wife wasn't rigid, and she realized that I wasn't irresponsible. We just looked at life through different lenses.

We also learned from that book that we process information differently. When I have a big decision to make, I'll process my thoughts out loud. Within five minutes, about 90 percent of my best thinking is out there. When I hear myself say something really stupid, I'm able to shift gears and verbalize another solution. But if someone listens to me trying to figure it out, they'll go nuts with what seems like indecision on my part. And if you're married to that kind of person, like Theresa is, it can be a little unsettling.

Theresa, on the other hand, processes information by being alone to think, pray, think some more, jot down some notes, and pray some more. So all of our back-and-forth about "why don't you just make a decision," "why are you clamming up," "I can't believe you're really considering that," and so on, was more a matter of different thought processes than different opinions. Acknowledging those differences, we were able to give each other room to think things through in our own way and then arrive at a decision together.

Many of my pastoral and leadership skills have also been developed through reading great books. In *The Effective Executive*, by Peter Drucker,[16] for example, I learned the difference between being effective and being efficient. Efficiency is doing things right; effectiveness is doing the right things. I realized that in ministry I needed to focus on effectiveness. That focus has shaped my priorities over the years.

Basic Theology, by Charles Ryrie, lays out the great doctrines of Scripture in their most simple form. *Explore the Book*, by J. Sidlow Baxter, gives an overview of every book in the Bible and weaves the theme of each book into the big picture of Scripture. *Methodical Bible Study*, by Robert Traina, has shaped how I do inductive Bible study.[17] I can't open the Bible without noticing how words are repeated or how paragraphs are structured or without making observations, interpretations, and applications about what I've read. The methods in that book have framed how I perceive Scripture.

Great Books Heal Your Soul

My first pastorate in Texas was miles from Dallas, far enough away to be considered out in the country. But quite a few people who lived there were business owners and entrepreneurs who had moved there to get away from city traffic and raise their kids in a calmer neighborhood. A church member could be wearing jeans and driving a pickup truck, but he was no more country than I am. In church business meetings I was surrounded by real estate investors, CPAs, and other business-savvy people.

As a twenty-eight-year-old pastor with a wife and three small kids, I felt out of my league.

I read a book by Paul Tournier, *The Strong and the Weak*,[18] which contained only one thesis and lots of illustrations to back it up. The thesis was that every person in the world, without exception, is desperately insecure. Some people cover up their insecurity with strong reactions and power trips, others try to intimidate, and many try to impress with what they wear, the car they drive, or the names they drop. At the opposite end of the spectrum are insecure people with weak reactions. They're overly shy, can't look you in the eye, and apologize for things that aren't even their fault.

As I read that book, I suddenly got a new pair of glasses with which to see the world. I remember going to a breakfast meeting with a powerful man who wore his influence on his sleeve. He always had to pay for the meal and have the last word. I had gotten to know some of his family and their issues, and as I sat back and observed him, I began to see him as a rich, powerful, strong, desperately insecure guy. He was just like me—not in the rich, powerful, and strong department, but in the insecurity I knew we both had. For the first time, instead of intimidation I felt compassion. He was struggling with life issues like I was, and his power plays were just an attempt to keep people away from those vulnerable and painful issues.

I began to look at everyone like that. A lot of what drives our decisions about what we say, what we wear, where we live, the schools we send our kids to, and everything else is related to fear of what people think of us. We cast an image of ourselves that we want people to believe. It's all about finding acceptance.

Once I realized that this is everyone's root problem, I knew the solution was to learn how accepted we are in Christ. That sets people free. When I sit with powerful, intimidating leaders now, I know where they're coming from, at least in general terms. The more pompous they get, the more insecure they are.

That changed my whole ministry. I noticed that I was most attracted to people who seem like average people with strengths and struggles who could be themselves around others. If that's the kind of person I was attracted to, that was probably the kind of person most other people are attracted to as well. Maybe, I thought, it would be good to be that kind of person.

When people tell me they appreciate my vulnerability and transparency in one of my messages, it isn't because I wanted to be vulnerable and transparent. I'm desperately insecure just like you are, and sometimes I would rather fake it and pretend to be strong and secure. But if I do that, I cast an image that isn't real, and then I have to deal with sin in my heart. But isn't the body of Christ the best place to get all that on the table and deal with it honestly and authentically? How else can life-change occur?

It's tragic that we've created a culture of phonies who are addicted to the approval of others. What we most need is love and acceptance, but we can't get them until we're really ourselves. Otherwise, the love and acceptance we think we're getting are based on a false image. Authentic living means accepting each other's pain and dysfunctions along with the successes and strengths. *The Strong and the Weak* changed how I saw people, and as a result, it profoundly transformed my ministry.

The Return of the Prodigal Son, by Henri Nouwen,[19] prompted a breakthrough in my late thirties. The greatest sin in the world, Nouwen says, is the sin of unbelief. It's the backdrop behind all the other sins we commit. And the unbelief we cling to most stubbornly is our refusal to accept that God loves us unconditionally. We don't understand that God's heart for us is not focused on how we perform, what we possess, who we impress, what we acquire, or what other people think. The prodigal son in Jesus's parable was at his absolute worst in terms of behavior and belief, and his father loved him totally, without regard to his works. It takes most of us years to let that move from our brains and sink into our hearts, but every time it moves in that direction, we get a little more free. We begin to read the Bible less as a rule book and more as a love letter written by a Father who wants the very best for us. That changes everything about how we pray and what we do.

Finally, *Abba's Child*, by Brennan Manning,[20] taught me the same theme from another angle. We have a false self and a true self, and we play all kinds of games in our minds to project the false self in order to protect the true self. But if we believe the acceptance and intimacy that's possible with our Father, it will transform our relationship with him, our view of ourselves, and how we relate to others.

Your Curriculum

You may be asking yourself why I've written so much about the actual content of these books rather than just telling you how important it is to find great ones and read them. After all, your experiences in life are different from mine; what has impacted me may have little effect on you and vice versa. But I've walked you through the books that have changed my life for a reason. I wanted you to see how the works and wisdom of some of the greatest men and women of God can be passed down to you through what they've written.

You probably won't want to go out and find every book I've read and expect them to affect you the same way they've affected me. This chapter isn't a class syllabus; you're free, with God's help, to find the books that will equip and empower you for the situations of your life. The important thing is not the titles I've mentioned but the practice of letting God transform your life through great teaching.

I hope you've gotten a good picture of how he has done that in my life. If you think back through those books that have profoundly changed me, you'll notice that these were not minor steps in my discipleship. In fact, they have taught me some huge life lessons. Books have shaped my perception of God, my confidence in the Bible, my marriage, my ministry, and my relationships with other people. They've done the same for countless other Christians throughout history, some of whom have impacted the kingdom of God on earth quite dramatically. If you took away the lessons these books have given me, I'd probably be left with a lot more struggles and a lot fewer breakthroughs. That's why I'll never regret the practice of reading great books. You won't either.

Action Steps

1. If you haven't already, begin developing a reading list of great Christian books. If you need suggestions, the titles in this chapter and recommendations from a pastor or church leader are a great place to start. Set a realistic goal that fits with your schedule—one book a month, for example—and plan two years' worth of reading.
2. Identify at least one of your current regular activities—like watching the evening news or surfing the Internet for an hour every day—that you could live without for a few weeks, and then try replacing that activity with the regular reading of quality Christian literature. After a few weeks, weigh the benefits of your new reading habit against the benefits of your former activity. If you sense God leading you to make that reading time permanent, do so. If not, try the experiment with another nonessential activity and see if God leads you to permanently replace that one with reading great books.
3. Memorize Nehemiah 8:8, "[The Levites] read from the Book of the Law of God, making it clear and giving the meaning so that the people could understand what was being read."

Questions for Reflection and Discussion

1. Do you think reading Christian books is an important discipline or simply a matter of personal interest? Why?
2. What book, other than the Bible, has had the most dramatic impact on your spiritual growth? What elements of that book made such a powerful impression on you? In what ways has God used the truths from that book in your life?
3. How do you think your life would change if you established a regular reading habit (or expanded one you already have)? How would it affect your schedule? your relationship with God? your long-term spiritual growth?

3

Pursue Great People

Elisha was persistent. His spiritual father and mentor was about to leave this life. As the prophet Elijah traveled from town to town toward the Jordan River, where God would send a chariot and a whirlwind to take him to heaven, Elisha insisted on following his friend all the way to the end.

"Stay here," Elijah kept saying to him.

"As surely as the LORD lives and as you live, I will not leave you," Elisha responded each time. And he followed him on the long journey, from town to town until they crossed the river.

Finally, Elisha issued a bold request: "Let me inherit a double portion of your spirit."

"You have asked a difficult thing," the older prophet responded. But if Elisha was able to see his master when he was taken up, the request would be granted (2 Kings 2:2–10).[1] So they walked together and talked until the chariot and the whirlwind came, and Elisha walked away with his mentor's mantle and a double portion of his spirit.

That's a great picture of an important spiritual truth: Who we choose to follow will determine, to a large degree, who we become. If we want to become great Christians, we need to pursue great Christians.

Sometimes great role models are right in front of us and easily accessible. Often they aren't. Great people, like Elijah, can be hard to follow, but persistence is almost always rewarded. We see this often in Scripture: Joshua was able to follow in Moses's footsteps because whenever Moses spoke with God "face to face" his young aide Joshua was near him drawing strength from the Lord's presence (Exod. 33:11). Solomon valued wisdom because his father, David, urged him to pursue understanding (Prov. 4:3–6). Timothy was encouraged and strengthened as a young pastor despite difficulties because he submitted himself to Paul's example and advice (2 Tim. 3:10–11; 1 Cor. 4:17; Phil. 2:22). And, most obviously, twelve men followed Jesus closely for three years, observing his works and listening to his words constantly. God puts great people in our lives so we can learn from them.

This isn't just a spiritual dynamic; it works in every area of knowledge and life. History is full of people who connected themselves to great people and eventually rose to their level of maturity. Whether it's a succession of philosophers (like Socrates mentoring Plato, who mentored Aristotle, who mentored Alexander the Great) or of kings (like the inherited power of most of the world's monarchies) or of apprenticed artisans of the Renaissance, a master's ceiling can become his disciple's floor if the disciple knows how to absorb the lessons of the master's life. God has ordained relationships as the primary medium for learning.

If that's true, doesn't it follow that we should learn from the best? If we want to become great in God's eyes, we need to learn from those who already are great. In order to move to the next level of discipleship and fruitfulness, we need to follow those who have already walked that path. They can lead us in the ways the Lord has taught them.

Before You Could Choose

A simple fact of human nature is that we will begin to take on the attributes of the people we spend the most time with.

The Bible is emphatic that we are shaped by the company we keep. As adults we get to choose our relational environment to a large degree, but none of us had anything to do with where we were born and who we spent the first few years of our life with. As a result, many of us inherit some extra baggage, and it can be very painful and discouraging. That makes it all the more important for us to seek out positive influences. Our baggage and our backgrounds demand that we pursue great people.

The most influential people in our lives, obviously, are our parents. For better or for worse, that's reality. We got whatever they had to offer in terms of both nature and nurture—genetically and environmentally. Our parents, or those who played the parental roles in our life, have shaped us more than anyone else has.

Before we move on to people we *choose* as life-shapers, we need to deal with those we didn't choose. Many people talk only about how wonderful their family was, and just as many talk only about the painful issues they've had to deal with because of what they went through in their family. The truth is that most of us are somewhere in the middle; we've been impacted both positively and negatively by parents and families. I've learned some important principles that have been helpful to me in dealing with family background issues.

1. *None of us had perfect parents*. We may find it easy to criticize our parents for not being perfect, and if we're not careful, we can hold grudges for actions or attributes we would easily forgive in another person. We started out thinking our parents were superheroes, and most of us have never gotten over the disappointment of finding out that they weren't. But Jesus was the only perfect person, so we grew up under the influence of imperfect people who made lots of mistakes. That's important to remember.

2. *Thank God for what we got rather than dwell on what we didn't get*. Most people go through a very normal, predictable phase in their twenties and thirties of lamenting what went wrong and what we missed out on with our parents. "My dad never said he loved me," or, "Mom was always very critical." Instead of focusing on what we did get, we focus on the negatives.

We forget that our parents didn't grow up in perfect families either, and they missed out on a lot because of their parents' weaknesses. That's part of being a member of the human race. We need to accept that fact and spend time instead thanking God for the blessings we did receive.

3. *Express appreciation for a lifetime.* Every human being, no matter how old, longs for a parent's approval. But most of us forget that our parents, no matter how old, long to hear a child's appreciation. Many of us have been through some very rough times and still carry resentments toward our parents, but we survived childhood and somehow were provided for. It isn't hard, once you're able to recognize the good things you received, to say, "Thanks, Mom; thanks, Dad."

4. *Deal constructively with the damage.* Everyone has baggage. Everyone went through difficult times. Not everyone, however, gets stuck there without ever learning to move on. Plenty of people come out of a bad situation and live a healthy, productive life. Be one of them. Deal constructively with whatever issues you have so you can grow. If you can pursue great lessons—however many or few there are—from the people God put in your life without your consent, you are well equipped to pursue great people of your own choosing.

Look in the Rearview Mirror

How do you know which great people to pursue? One of the first steps is to look in the rearview mirror. Which four or five people have most positively impacted your life? When you look back to see how and why God used certain people to develop your character, you begin to notice patterns. You get a glimpse of your individual needs and start to understand the kind of people you'll need to have in your life in the future.

That's why it's important to develop your own spiritual "Mount Rushmore." In other words, identify those few people whose influence in your life is positive and indelible—the people you'll always remember because they inspired you and taught you about life. They can be role models, mentors, teachers,

big brothers and sisters, friends, Christians, non-Christians—
whomever God has used to shape you. As you reflect on the four
or five key players in your history, you'll stir up memories of
the lessons they taught you. You'll also see more clearly where
they left off and where you need to find new great people to
pursue.

My Spiritual Mount Rushmore

You need someone who believes in you, who will speak the
truth in love, who can give you a picture of the kind of person
you want to be, and who will help you set goals and push you
toward them. Five people have played that role for me, and
they make up my spiritual Mount Rushmore.

Coach Lantz

"Ingram, get in here now!"

When Coach Lantz leaned out of his office window and yelled
your name for the whole locker room to hear, you knew you
were in trouble. And you knew you better get in there—sooner
than *now*.

I hurried into his office. He looked around and then shut
the door, grabbed me by my T-shirt, and seated me firmly in
the chair. My eyes were as big as saucers. These were the days
before anybody worried about a teacher giving a spanking, and
I had no idea what was going to happen next.

Coach got down in my face. "Ingram, I've got to tell you
something. I'm hearing things about you, and your big mouth
is going to get you in trouble. Next year you're going up to high
school, and I think you could really do something with your
life. But you're so arrogant and mouthy, if you keep popping
off like that you're going to end up with some teeth missing.
You understand, Ingram?"

"Yes, Coach."

Coach Lantz knew how to get my attention. He was my first
nonfamily role model. He was the kind of guy we all wanted

to be like. He was young, he was fun, and he could really play basketball. But he was hard on me and wouldn't let me get away with being a mouthy, arrogant kid, even if I was that way because I was so insecure. He looked past my surface behavior and saw some potential begging to be cultivated.

Every day at noon, Coach would play one-on-one with me. "Chip, get your elbow in; no, that's not what you do here; stay low. . . ." I got individual time with a man who believed in me and showed me what it looked like to be strong. I learned that you have to be teachable and quit trying to impress people. Coach cared enough to look underneath the hood, see some potential, and draw it out of me.

My relationship with Coach Lantz lasted long after junior high. I painted houses with him for five or six years. We'd have long talks about life and everything in it. Even after I had gone to college, Coach drove for hours to sit in the stands and watch me play. When I hadn't played well, he'd tell me how I needed to think and what I could do to get my confidence back. He invested quite a bit of his time working with me, sharing his wisdom with me, and, as in the above example, bluntly challenging me about issues that were keeping me from becoming the man God wanted me to be. He took the time to learn how I was wired, and he knew when to encourage and when to confront. His coaching extended far beyond basketball and helped prepare me for life. More than anyone else outside my home, Coach Lantz shaped me during my teenage years.

Punkie

Another one of my role models was my sister, Punkie. She taught me what it's like to be a Christian. Not many brother-sister relationships are like ours was. She was barely a year older than me, but when I'd come in from playing basketball, she would ask if I was hungry and fix me a sandwich. When my friends came over to watch a ball game, she'd pour some drinks for us. She showed me what a servant heart looks like.

About midway through high school, Punkie got involved with Campus Crusade and came to Christ. She never preached or nagged at me, but her example had a powerful influence. I remember being with a group of guys who were going out drinking, and the question in my mind was not what God would think—I didn't know him yet—and it wasn't what my parents would think. My number one question was what Punkie would think. I didn't want to let her down. I had never had anyone model love and integrity for me like she did.

Everyone needs a role model for Christian character—someone who demonstrates the person of Christ in everyday life. Punkie was a kind and winsome Christian, and I wanted to be like her.

Dave Marshall

My third major role model was a guy named Dave Marshall. Dave isn't my coach, a teacher, or a family member. He's a brick-layer with a high school education. Dave had been trained by the Navigators and wanted to see God work on the small campus where I attended college. He had a heart for discipleship.

The first time I met Dave was when I went with a friend to a Bible study at his home. It was open to the whole campus, but only four or five people were there. Dave opened the door, and I was not impressed with his style. He was one of the least cool people I had ever met. He got a guitar out, the few of us who were there sang some songs to Jesus, and I was wondering what in the world I'd gotten myself into. But the friend I had come with—a fullback on the football team—said it was cool and insisted I come back again and again.

Within a month, Dave had taught me how to have a quiet time, even though I was a reluctant learner. He taught me how to memorize verses, looking them up in the Bible and writing them in the blanks in a workbook. After a while, he said, "Chip, there are some guys on this campus who don't know the Lord. Why don't we go talk to them?" I was terribly embarrassed to be witnessing with an uncool guy, but people responded to him because he was so loving. During college, and later when I moved to teach school and helped Dave launch a new campus ministry, this self-taught man showed me what it looked like to make disciples.

Dave was all substance—not showy, not external, just authentic. Those Bible studies in his home were not the most exciting I've ever been in, but they were consistent. He opened the Bible, we read it together, and he taught me. I saw a consistent pattern for discipleship from someone who was steady and faithful.

I remember watching Dave at a county fair as he let a Jehovah's Witness and a Mormon get tied into a doctrinal pretzel rather than letting them tie him into one. As he pointed out what God's Word really teaches, they shook their heads and said, "Wow, I didn't know that was in the Bible." There was no hint of criticism or judgment, just gentle but firm love. He knew God's Word and he lived it.

All the Scripture memory and witnessing were great training for me, but most of what I learned from Dave came from watching his life. I lived in an apartment above his garage and spent many holiday breaks and summers with him and his family because he wanted to invest his life in me. His home was different than the one I grew up in. I didn't come from a Christian home where we prayed and read the Bible. We went to church sometimes, but we didn't talk about God. But as I watched this bricklayer with his wife and their four young kids, I caught a vision for the kind of life I wanted to live.

I remember seeing Dave come down the stairs one Thursday night in a suit and tie, his cologne announcing his presence before he even came into view. It wasn't a natural look—or smell—for him.

"Dave, what in the world are you doing?" I asked.

"I'm going on a date."

"With who?"

"Who do you think?" he said. "Polly."

And I watched this man go on a date every Thursday night with his wife of twenty-plus years. I watched him sit at the breakfast table and read the Bible with his kids and listened to him pour out his heart in prayer years later when one of them went through a rebellious phase. After a Christian conference one weekend, I saw him stop in a driving rain to lie in the mud and fix a guy's car as all the hotshots who had taught at the conference drove on by. He didn't make much money, but he gave sacrificially and brought missionaries into his house. People waited for months or even a year for him to do their chimney because he had such a good reputation. When we built foundations together, if they were a quarter of an inch off, he wasn't satisfied. I got an up-close view of a man of excellence and integrity.

Dave was a 2 Timothy 2:2 kind of guy: "The things which you have heard from me in the presence of many witnesses, entrust these to faithful men who will be able to teach others also" (NASB). I learned that life is not about flash or big events. It's about faithful, godly people getting up and putting one foot ahead of the other, fighting through the routines of life, doing the right thing by honoring commitments. I saw the fruit of his ministry: scores of people he discipled are now in full-time ministry, with some on every continent on Earth.

Today Dave is working with Chinese students doing their doctoral work in West Virginia. He says he's getting too old for college students, so he's moved on to graduate students. He teaches himself what he needs to know to relate to them, and he's seeing some of the most brilliant minds from an atheistic background come to know Christ.

Years ago, I realized deep in my heart that I wanted to be a man like Dave Marshall. I wanted a marriage like his, I wanted to be a dad like he is, and I wanted to be able to handle God's Word like he does.

Howard Hendricks

The final mentor I'll mention is Howard Hendricks, a well-known professor at Dallas Seminary. Whenever Prof finished teaching, I'd feel like getting up and running out the door to do God's will. I had never heard anyone communicate with such power, and I could tell there was something about his life that I wanted reproduced in mine, so I took every class he taught.

"Prof, I'd like to spend some time with you," I said one day. He told me about his busy travel schedule and recommended that I first get in a small group and make sure I was doing the basics. So I got in a small group, and six months later, I made an appointment to see him.

"Prof, I'd like to spend some time with you," I told him again. And again he told me how busy he was and how he could only spend time with a few people—those who were in a small group *and* who were majoring in Christian education. I changed my major, and six months later I went to him again.

"Prof, I'd like to spend some time with you." Again, he told me about all the demands on his schedule, but this time he offered the possibility of coming to his home whenever he was hosting a high-profile speaker or a missionary for an informal get-together. I got the dates from the secretary and put them on my calendar, and whenever his home was open for the next couple of years, Theresa and I were there.

Eventually, I pushed for more time with him, and he finally agreed that I could go along with him when he spoke at a conference—*if* I could pay my own airfare. Most seminary students don't make much money, and Theresa and I were living in government-subsidized housing. But I started saving money and was able to buy a plane ticket for a pastors' conference in Indiana where Dr. Hendricks was speaking.

I prepared for the flight by writing on an index card the fifteen questions I most wanted to ask him. I assumed that Dr. Hendricks had as electric a presence and as talkative a personality as he did when speaking in front of large groups, only to discover on the flight that he's not really into chit-chat in his personal time. I hit him with my fifteen questions, and within ten minutes we were done talking. Finally his wife, Jean, leaned over and began asking me questions about my family and plans for the future. She and I got to know each other for the next two or three hours. Then as he taught his material at the conference, I put all of his notes on the overhead projector at the right time. At his meetings, I'd be next to him to help him with whatever he needed. And when Jean left the conference a couple of days before it ended, I got to move into his hotel room and spend some time with him there.

As I assisted Prof by carrying his folders around that week, my desire to peek at his teaching notes was irresistible. I mean, how is a zealous student with aspirations of preaching and teaching supposed to resist inside information from a guy he considers the best teacher in the world? I had been learning from my classes, but at times I felt like I was being put in a straitjacket. Typing out every word of my sermons was making me nuts. So I asked Prof about his notes.

"Prof, what does 'boat story' mean?"

"It means that's where I tell my boat story," he answered.

"What are all these highlights and underlines of phrases that aren't even complete sentences?"

"Those are the things I want to emphasize when I preach this message."

"Aren't you supposed to write it all out like they're teaching us at school?"

"Look, Chip, they're teaching you the fundamentals," he said. "You have to know the basics before you let your gift come through in its own way. You'll eventually develop your own style. When I tell a story, I picture in my mind what happened and describe it like I'm there. That's what works for me."

"That's legal?"

"Sure. You've got to be comfortable with your delivery."

In the mornings, Prof got up and studied the Bible for an hour. He chose one book to study each month, and he went through it again and again, charted it out, and thought his way through it more and more deeply. And I understood why he knew Scripture better than anyone I had ever met.

Each night before going to sleep, Dr. Hendricks would say, "Hey, you want to pray?"

"Sure," I'd answer. Then we knelt on the floor, and I realized that the heart of his communication wasn't about his gift for teaching or about being a famous author. It was his passion for God. I felt like I went to the Holy of Holies when he prayed. I understood what gripped his heart and how it poured through to his students. I got to overhear a man of God talk with his Lord.

Probably the biggest highlight for me was one night, long after we had turned out the lights, when we talked about a struggle I was having. I hadn't shared it with anyone yet, and I didn't know how to solve it. I lay there wondering how open I should be and what he would think of me for pouring my heart out. But I was getting more comfortable around him, so I shared my problem and explained that I couldn't figure out how to resolve it. He assured me that everyone had those kinds of struggles and openly shared from his heart about how he had come through some of his personal battles. Then he gave me a few suggestions and told me about someone who could help walk me through it. It was one of those late-night conversations where you finally look at the clock and can't believe how late it is, and it helped start a relationship that has lasted for decades.

Prof has visited the churches I've pastored, he prays for me, and he has served on the board of directors at Walk Thru the Bible. God has used him to change my life and develop my heart and my skills as a pastor and teacher.

That's what it means to pursue great people. You figure out who can help you the most, and you find a way into their life. You can go ahead and assume that they're busy and over-whelmed and probably don't have time for you. But they have time for *some* people, and your job is to find out how to be one of them. Sometimes they'll tell you that they just can't fit you in, so you wait. Maybe in a year or two they'll have more time, or maybe God will point you to someone else. But one way or another, you can put yourself under a mentor like I put myself under Dr. Hendricks. Sure, I made a pest of myself at first, but eventually God opened the door into the life of a man who has been a friend and mentor for thirty years now.

Theresa

The central face on my Mount Rushmore is my wife. More than any professor, more than any book, more than any men-tor or disciple maker, Theresa has had the greatest influence on my life. I could go on for days about her, but I'll just give you some highlights.

Theresa has impacted me most by her integrity. She is the most honest person I know—at times to the point of being a real pain. Nothing gets by. It has to be right; it has to be honest; it has to be truthful. Exaggeration and white lies are not in her vocabulary, and she has been a much-needed balance to my "that's close enough" personality.

Next is her devotion to God. Like many, I dated a number of people before I found Theresa. By the time I was really looking for a wife, I realized that all the superficial attributes guys look for in a woman come and go, but God doesn't see as we do. "Man looks at the outward appearance, but the LORD looks at the heart" (1 Sam. 16:7). And while I was certainly attracted to Theresa outwardly, I was also drawn to what's in her heart. It has been a powerful experience for over twenty-five years to see her passion for Christ and watch someone get up at 5:30 and start every day praying. I see how much time she spends in the Bible and how she has fasted and prayed for our kids when they were going through difficult times. Her life of devotion has challenged and inspired me deeply.

Theresa may be cute and petite, but she also models strength and courage. One of the things a coach looks for in players is mental toughness. There are times in a ballgame when you can watch two teams with players whose legs are tired, and they are getting worn down. But those who are able to reach down deep inside and refuse to quit will eventually come out on top. My wife has more of that than any player I ever coached or any teammate I've ever played with. I have taken her across the United States, around the world, and away from home and family. Has she ever struggled? Of course. But she's never wavered.

The final characteristics that have powerfully affected my life have been her consistency and follow-through. You know those little meetings spouses have where you talk about plans for the budget, the kids, or lifestyle decisions? When we write down a plan on paper, she follows it through—consistently and persistently. Her integrity, mental toughness, courage, strength, and resolve have helped develop those qualities in me. Apart from Christ, she has been the most influential person in my life.

Who are the people in your life who have shaped you? Proverbs 27:17 says, "As iron sharpens iron, so one man sharpens another." The Bible is very clear about the benefits and the necessity of positive, close relationships. It tells us not to forsake gathering together to spur each other on to love and good works (Heb. 10:24–25). "Encourage one another daily, . . . so that none of you may be hardened by sin's deceitfulness" (Heb. 3:13). And Proverbs 13:20 gives us both a great promise and a strong warning: "He who walks with the wise grows wise, but a companion of fools suffers harm."

Look Out the Windshield

When you've looked in the rearview mirror and reflected on your Mount Rushmore of great influences, you have a better idea of whom to pursue next. You can look out the windshield and see the people God has placed on your horizon, knowing that he put some of them there to mold you into the person he wants you to be.

Prof once said something I'll never forget: "Chip, everyone needs a Paul, a Timothy, and a Barnabas in their life—a Paul to learn from as a mentor and role model, a Timothy to sow seeds into the next generation with teaching and encouragement, and a Barnabas you can be totally open with, an encouraging friend who will go through life with you in the good times and in the sweat and heartache. That will keep you balanced." That's not a bad way to think of what it means to pursue great people. You need to have role models, and you need to be one.

These relationships don't always need to be long-term, and they don't always need to be formalized. Variety is not only acceptable, it's advisable. I have one Paul who has a doctorate and another who has only a high school education. Great people don't fit into a box; they'll often stretch your expectations. You aren't necessarily looking for someone who's famous or popular. Look to see in his or her life the kinds of things that make you think, "In my heart of hearts, I want to grow in that area."

Paul

A. C. is one of my Pauls. He became like a dad to me. He helped me paint the bathroom in the first house of the first pastorate I had—a church with about thirty-five people. In that bathroom, we dreamed a great dream together. Our little church building was fifteen miles outside a little town with no traffic lights, and we were dreaming about building a church with a thousand members that would transform Kauffman, Texas (population 4,500). A. C. didn't laugh. He believed God could work through us like that, and about eight years later we had a church of five hundred people. God had me move on at that point, but we wouldn't have gotten that far if we hadn't dreamed a great dream and if A. C. hadn't encouraged me to pursue it.

I was able to share my struggles with him—marital issues, parenting problems, difficult relationships in the church, and so on. More than twenty years later, he's still a father and a mentor. I asked him to be on the board of Living on the Edge, and then when I moved to Walk Thru the Bible, he came on the board there. I'm still learning from him and being encouraged by him.

Bill was an engineer, one of the brightest and most focused people I've ever known. He had responsibility in a major company for the entire region east of the Mississippi River. He came to Christ as an adult and was able to study five or six hours a night during the weeks he traveled.

I learned from Bill what devotion looks like. I've never met a man more sensitive to the Lord. Every Thursday night when he was in town, we went out and shared Christ with people who had visited the church. One night we were talking with a woman who understood the gospel but showed no desire to commit to Jesus. I don't like rejection—no one does—and I was ready to move on to the next person. But I watched Bill, a very large man with a black belt in judo, as tears began to stream down his face. He turned to the woman and said, "You need to understand that the decision you're making is a decision for a Christless eternity, and the God of heaven who loves you gave his Son for you. I just want you to know you're rejecting him and what the consequences are. And I want you to know that we love you." Bill taught me what it means to speak the truth in love, even when it's uncomfortable.

Later we had a very sticky situation in the church that involved sexual indiscretion and a man living a double life, and it required real church discipline. Bill and I were responsible for confronting this man. We had all the substantiated information, and we knew the truth about the situation. But it's hard to be courageous in cases like that, especially as a young pastor. It's easy to say about 90 percent of what needs to be said and then, when encountering resistance, let the conversation end without resolution.

Bill must have known what I needed as an inexperienced pastor. He opened the conversation, laid out the whole situation, and explained how a Christian's life needs to be consistent. I sat there thinking, "Bill, you're doing a great job." Then he looked right at this guy who had just been confronted with his very deviant behavior and said, "Chip wants to tell you how we're going to deal with this." Bill knew that unless a pastor learns to step up, be a man, and shoot it straight, he risks missing out on many ways God wants to use him. He modeled for me what it means to be both sensitive to people's needs and uncompromising with truth, and I've never forgotten it.

Barnabas

One of my Barnabases is a fellow named Glen. He and I met playing ball overseas, and we've been friends for about thirty years. We bonded like David and Jonathan, and I know he still prays for me regularly. We know when to encourage each other and when to challenge each other.

On a ministry trip together once, Glen said, "What book of the Bible do you want to memorize? We've got three weeks."

I was arrogant enough not to say, "Are you kidding me? A whole book?" So instead, I said something like, "Sure, let's do Philippians." And the next morning he quoted the first half of the first chapter, and I realized I needed to get on the ball. He wasn't legalistic about it; he had a winsome, devoted attitude. He just lives what he believes. He would break out into spontaneous songs on the bus, joyful about life. I've never been more spiritually challenged.

Timothy

One of my Timothys, who later turned into a Barnabas, is a guy named Steve, an All-American defensive back at Austin

Peay College. He came on staff in our small church and later moved with me to California. I've shared everything with Steve; I hope he never decides to write a book about me. Of course, I'm sure he doesn't want me to write a book about him either. We've been extremely honest with each other.

That's probably Steve's greatest gift to me. He has been brutally honest, to the point that people have thought he was mad at me. The more God gives you a public platform, the more you need people who are totally and completely unimpressed, and Steve has ignored what anyone else thinks of me and has loved me for me. He's one of the safest people in the world because I only have to be Chip around him.

Getting Started without Getting Discouraged

I've learned over the years that when you look for Pauls and Timothys, you can get quite discouraged if you don't heed a couple of warnings. First, if you're a Timothy looking for a Paul, don't expect to find that one perfect person who will meet that need for the rest of your life. God will probably use a variety of people—none of them perfect, but all with something to offer—at different seasons in your life. Since no one is the complete package, he may bring mentors and role models into your life through a revolving door. That's normal.

Second, if you're a Paul looking for a Timothy, don't let yourself get into a position of always giving and never receiving. If you're pouring yourself into one person, let someone else—or even that same person—pour something back into you. Otherwise, you'll lose the joy of being a Christian and wonder why you're tired all the time. You need some VEPs in your life: Very Encouraging People. Give yourself permission to be renewed and to have fun. Have some relationships that have no agenda other than just hanging out. Let yourself be refreshed.

Keep your relationships in perspective. Learn to recognize what God wants you to get from them. Some people will play the role of a father or mother figure. God will put others in your life simply to be a cheerleader or a confidant. At various times you'll need a hero, a prophet, a sponsor, an expert, and a counselor. When you understand the different purposes God has for the people around you, it will help you not be offended when a prophet confronts you, for example, or increase your motivation when a sponsor pushes you.

In order to pursue great people, you'll need to:

- *Pray earnestly.* God is involved in your spiritual growth; ask him persistently and zealously to put people around you who can fulfill every role you need.
- *Take initiative.* Great people aren't likely to come to you. More often than not, you'll need to go to them.
- *Start in your relational network.* Most of the people God wants to use in your life are already there. You may need to expand your network on occasion, but he'll start with the people he's placed around you.
- *Ask for help.* No one grows spiritually or any other way without needing advice. No matter who you are or how much experience you have, you'll be in over your head sometimes in this life, and you'll need to ask for help.
- *Persevere.* Pursuing great people is not a momentary appeal. Pursuit implies effort and time. Don't give up if a relationship doesn't develop the way you want it to at first. Give it time and keep trying.
- *Do it by proxy.* Not every great Christian you pursue will be accessible in person all the time. Some of them, in fact, may have lived long before you were born. You can learn from great people through books, recordings, and, if distance is the only obstacle, by phone.
- *Make time in your schedule.* You'll never *have* enough time to pursue great people. As with almost everything that's important in life, you'll have to *make* time.

I encourage you to pursue great people because, for better or worse, you will be shaped by the people around you. Whomever you hang out with, whoever's teaching you come under, and whomever you choose to influence you will greatly determine the direction of your life. If you want to be an average Christian, surround yourself with average Christians. If, however, you want to go from good to great in God's eyes, surround yourself with great people.

Action Steps

1. Remind yourself several times this week that pursuing great people is a process. It involves earnest prayer and initiative on your part. You'll need to ask for help at times and be able to persevere.
2. Develop your own spiritual Mount Rushmore. Make a list of the four or five people who have had the most beneficial and lasting impact on your life, and then describe which of their characteristics had a powerful effect on you and why. If your Mount Rushmore seems incomplete, ask God to bring people into your life who can fill out the picture.
3. Identify at least one area of your life in which you know you need significant growth. Is there anyone currently in your relational network who can help you in that area? Conversely, identify at least one area of your life in which you know God has given you much encouragement and strength. Is there anyone currently in your relational network who needs your help in that area? If the answer to either question is *yes*, take at least one step this week to get closer to that person (or people).
4. Memorize 2 Timothy 2:2, "The things you have heard me say in the presence of many witnesses entrust to reliable men who will also be qualified to teach others."

Questions for Reflection and Discussion

1. What obstacles might stand in the way of pursuing great people? How natural is it for you to invite yourself into someone else's life? What advice would you give people who are not naturally outgoing to help them pursue great people?

2. Is there anyone in your life who functions as a coach? a role model? an encourager? a completely honest friend? Which relationship do you think is most important for you right now? How can you know when to pursue a great person to help you?

3. Is there anyone in your life right now who needs you as a coach? a role model? an encourager? a completely honest friend? Do you think God has placed you near someone to meet a specific need in his or her development?

4

Dream Great Dreams

The young man dedicated his whole life to one dream: playing pro basketball. He drilled himself, practicing eight to twelve hours a day so he could play college ball on a scholarship. Even as early as the sixth grade, he had dreamed of being the first player to earn a million-dollar salary. That was unheard of in those days, but dreams don't confine themselves to what has already been done. This dreamer saw great possibilities.

In college, he averaged forty-three points a game his sophomore year and forty-four his junior and senior years. Those numbers are amazing, much more so in the era before the three-point shot was part of the game. He became the NBA's top draft pick, the first player to be paid a seven-figure salary, and the youngest inductee into the basketball Hall of Fame. His dream turned into reality.

I remember reading Pete Maravich's story in *Sports Illustrated* when I was about eight. I had a similar dream, and I caught his vision for how to accomplish it. I saw how he had dedicated himself, so I began to do the drills he did—behind-the-back passes, between-the-legs dribbling, endless free-throws, and shots from every angle imaginable. I usually played ball at least eight hours a day, sometimes as many as eleven or twelve. Even when I watched TV, I'd go through the mechanics of a jump shot. I was obsessive about it and very, very focused.

I was under five feet tall when I was in seventh grade, but that's one of those details dreams ignore. My freshman year in high school I was only five-four. Didn't matter. Suggestions to try out for the wrestling team didn't register with me. I couldn't let dating get in the way either, callously breaking up with a great girl the night before basketball season started. I persevered through setbacks, set my clock around basketball, established a healthy diet, and brushed aside every distraction. I was determined, and nothing—absolutely nothing—could get in the way of my dream.

When you're driven by a dream like that, it shapes everything you do. I can't say today that my dream was the right one, or even a good one. Obviously, my dreams have changed drastically over the years. But that sense of absolute commitment to a goal has stuck with me. And even though my dream seems small in retrospect, it paid for my college education. It also gave me an opportunity to travel with an evangelistic basketball team and share Christ with people in nearly every country in South America and East Asia. It has shaped my life in ways I could not have imagined.

Great accomplishments usually begin with the pursuit of a dream. Some dreamers, like Pete Maravich, accomplish exactly the goals they set out to accomplish. Others, like me, are redirected along the way as God refines and shapes their passion. Either way, the future is shaped by the visions held dear in the hearts of human beings.

There is tremendous power in a dream. When you believe a picture of the future, and that picture bleeds out of your heart—not because you have to or ought to accomplish it, but because you intensely *want* to—it blows wind in your sails and directs the course of your life. It can also direct the course of history.

Quite a few dreams have done that, both positively and negatively. Alexander the Great dreamed of ruling the world, and his conquests have shaped Western civilization forever. (Our

New Testament, for example, is written in Greek because of his empire's expansion.) Persecuted Christians and political malcontents dreamed of a land of protection and freedom, and their colonial territories in the Americas have flourished before and after independence. Hitler dreamed of establishing the superiority of his race, and the resulting war devastated half the world, deeply scarred the Jewish people, and shaped the political landscape to this day. Martin Luther King dreamed of a society without racism, and his efforts helped define a movement that radically altered American culture for the better. (It's no coincidence that King's greatest speech is best known for this one phrase: "I have a dream.") A dream, whether for good or for evil, whether of an individual or a group, can be a mighty influence.

We see the same dynamic in church history. Paul dreamed of preaching Christ before philosophers and emperors, and the church spread throughout Asia and Europe. William Carey dreamed of taking the gospel to India, and an entire missions movement was born. Hudson Taylor dreamed of reaching China's interior with the gospel, and the underground Chinese church is flourishing today. Dwight Moody had a dream for the youth of Chicago and ended up launching a church, establishing a network of schools, starting a Bible college, and cultivating an evangelistic movement. Those are just a few examples among very many throughout history. Great works almost always begin with great dreams.

What is your dream? It doesn't matter if you're seven or seventy; your heart should be captivated by a vision of how to serve God and accomplish something for his kingdom. If you're like many, you may have disowned your dream long ago as "unrealistic" or "impractical," and perhaps it was. But there was some element of it that God put within you, something he wants to use to inspire and direct you.

Many of the elements of being great in God's eyes will point toward this principle. Thinking great thoughts, reading great books, pursuing great people, and the other characteristics of greatness we'll cover later will cultivate God-given dreams and give you practical means to accomplish them. To fulfill his purposes and build his kingdom, God will first and foremost direct his energy toward one thing: captivating your heart with great dreams.

The Impossible Dream

He said it with a straight face. An eclectic group of ordinary men gathered around him, as they had done for the better part of three years, and listened attentively to the words of this one remarkable person. And without apologies or lengthy explanations, this is what he told them: "All power in heaven and earth has been given to me. Now go reach the entire planet. That's your mission."

Within the first hundred years, the church nearly reached the goal of spreading the gospel to the known world. Thomas went as far as India, according to many. Paul was on his way to Spain. Other early believers went south into Africa and north into Asia. After only three centuries, a powerful, secular, corrupt culture was turned upside down and the Christian faith became its dominant worldview.

Twelve ordinary, uneducated people began that mission without a printing press, without TVs and DVD players, and without the Internet. There was no marketing campaign, ad agency, or strategic plan, other than the inspiration of the Spirit and sensitivity to his leading. Most of the impetus for the spread of the faith came only from a profound commitment to the words of Jesus and some really sanctified dreaming.

God delights to do . . .
impossible things
through *improbable* people
to impart *exceeding* grace
to *undeserving* recipients.

I believe this fits perfectly with the heart of God. When I read through the pages of Scripture, I see a God who delights to do impossible things through improbable people and to impart exceeding grace to undeserving recipients.

Think about that. God established his people through the unlikely pregnancy of a very old couple. He parted a huge body of water so his people could walk through it. He took a tiny nation and made it the center of the world. He whittled Gideon's army down to a fraction of its size to defeat a formidable foe. He used a shepherd with a slingshot to slay a malicious giant. He preserved his people through the petitions of Esther, a most unlikely queen with a risky request. He unveiled the message of the eternal mystery of salvation through common fishermen, ex-prostitutes, and ex-swindlers. And don't forget, he accomplished a cosmic victory through a man who was born in a stable and executed on an instrument of torture.

That means that your dreams are not too unlikely for God, and you are not too improbable for him to use. In fact, he enjoys accomplishing his purposes through dreams that are unlikely and improbable. He especially delights in doing the impossible through people who, by faith, didn't think their dream was impossible at all. Those who grasp the immensity of God's power can have dreams without limits.

But God must be the source not only of fulfillment but of the dream to begin with. Dreams are not about your self-fulfillment or self-actualization, and they have nothing to do with whether you become famous. God *wants* you to be fulfilled, of course, but only he knows the best way to accomplish that. He invites ordinary people to dream something so great that it would be impossible if God did not do it. He wants your heart to be filled with dreams that are far bigger than you are—*his* dreams for *his* purposes so that you and he can delight in them together forever. I call this sanctified, God-honoring dreaming.

The Basis of Sanctified Dreaming

We've somehow bought into the idea that people who do great things for God are specially gifted with unusual talents and capabilities. Usually just the opposite is true. They are ordinary people who have allowed God to do something extraordinary in them. They bank on the fact that all things are possible with God and allow their minds to explore the possibilities. A sanctified imagination—dreams that are born from the intimate communion between Jesus and his people—is the fuel that gets kingdom business done. Great dreams are birthed when we begin to believe that:

1. God Is Able

This is an unusual concept for many people, so let me give you some scriptural background before we go any further. First, if our God is going to partner with us in impossible endeavors, we need to understand that he is able to accomplish anything. As Jeremiah 32:17 says, "You have made the heavens and the earth by Your great power and by Your outstretched arm! Nothing is too difficult for You" (NASB).

Think of the most difficult situation in your life—a problem that seems unmovable. It isn't too difficult for God. It isn't even *mildly* difficult. Or think of the most outrageous dream you can imagine. Again, it's not too hard for him. Not even close. There is no set of circumstances that puts him in a bind or makes him wish he'd done things differently. He is able to resolve anything at any time.

2. God Is Desirous

Not only is he able to do big things through us, he's willing. He wants to do "things which eye has not seen and ear has not heard, and which have not entered the heart of man, all that God has prepared for those who love him" (1 Cor. 2:9 NASB). Doesn't that sound like a God who wants to do great things? This verse is often used at funerals to remind grieving people of the hope we have in Christ, but I believe it also applies to life here and now. We can't come up with a dream too big for God, and he has given us every reason to believe he wants us to raise our level of expectation.

We often try to lower our expectations and quiet our dreams because we feel that they are too unrealistic or that God wouldn't do something huge through insignificant people like us. But those issues don't limit God. In fact, we have a Bible full of examples of him doing unrealistic things through improbable people. Our self-imposed limitations are a lot like Mary's question to the angel Gabriel when he announced that Jesus would be born through her. She is perplexed that an angel has come to see her (Luke 1:29)—like us, she feels she is an unlikely recipient of a miracle. Then she wonders how it is possible. Gabriel's answer? "Nothing is impossible with God" (Luke 1:37).

3. God Has Promised

Not only is God able, and not only does he want to, he also promised. Psalm 37:4 has often been used as a self-help verse, but the heart of it is something entirely different: "Delight yourself in the LORD and he will give you the desires of your heart." In other words, get so consumed and in love with God, so overwhelmed with who he is and what he does, that your delight in him births all sorts of desires that he would be zealous to fulfill. When we get an awesome, inspiring view of God, our hearts begin to beat like his. In that communion, dreams rise up and are fulfilled.

Our biggest problem isn't that our dreams are too big; it's that they're too small.

Imagine having a dream for all the unwed mothers in your city, or for feeding every person who otherwise wouldn't eat today, or for reaching high-income executives or ends-of-the-earth tribes with the gospel. Do you think God would be behind any of those dreams? Would he be interested in giving you the desires of your heart?

I think he would. So why don't we see more dreams fulfilled? I'm convinced that the reason is not that people are dreaming big and ending up disappointed because God didn't come through. The problem is that few people are dreaming like that. Most of us look at our desk calendars and try to figure out how to get everything done this week that we need to do. We focus on the now, the narrow, the next step in our survival. God wants us to lift our eyes beyond that. Our biggest problem isn't that our dreams are too big; it's that they're too small.

4. God Invites Us

Finally, in addition to being assured of God's ability, his desire, and his promise, we also have an open invitation. Psalm 2 is a messianic psalm—a Psalm that prophesies about Jesus—but its words were an invitation to Israel and now to all who are in Christ. The invitation in verse 8 is astounding: "Ask of Me, and I will surely give the nations as Your inheritance, and the very ends of the earth as Your possession" (NASB).

In other words, God isn't thinking in small terms. If he put such a big dream in his Word and invited his people into that dream, surely he also encourages us today to look at the big picture. The all-powerful God who holds billions of galaxies in his hands tells his Son and those who follow him that all they have to do is ask—to dream a great, godly dream and go after it—and he will go so far as to give them the nations as their inheritance. That's an amazing invitation.

That's why Jesus is able to give his disciples the kinds of promises we memorize for encouragement. In John 14, for example, after Jesus has washed the disciples' feet and promised them that the Comforter will come, he blows their minds with these words:

> Truly, truly, I say to you, he who believes in Me, the works that I do, he will do also; and greater works than these he will do; because I go to the Father. Whatever you ask in My name, that will I do, so that the Father may be glorified in the Son. If you ask Me anything in My name, I will do it.
>
> John 14:12–14 NASB

When Jesus says "truly, truly," he really wants to make a point. It means "most assuredly" or "this is an absolute certainty." Can you imagine the disciples' amazement when Jesus told them they would most assuredly be able to do the works that he did? All the miracles of healing, deliverance, and raising the dead, all the works of compassion and mercy, all the wisdom and teaching that he did would now be carried out by these ordinary men. Not only that, Jesus tells them that they would do even *greater* works than his.

What condition is between the lines of this blank check of a promise? Only that his disciples abide in him (John 15:4, 6, 9 NASB)—that their hearts be his, their minds be on his kingdom, and their fellowship with him be genuine, and that they ask in his name and for his glory.

Look Who's Talking

The context of Jesus's words is obviously his earthly ministry, but think for a moment about the one who made this promise of "greater works." Colossians 1:15–20 gives us a picture of the deity of Jesus, especially with regard to creation. He's the one who spoke this universe into being. Everything that exists was created by him and for him.

Do you realize how mind-stretching that is? Let me give you a few facts about the world we live in. Our planet flies around the sun at sixty-seven thousand miles per hour. Each year, its journey is completed at precisely the same speed, virtually down to the second. This massive planet on this long journey is hidden in a sea of some 200 billion stars in the galaxy. And scientists estimate this galaxy is nestled among more than 125 billion galaxies. When we try to calculate the number of stars or the distances across space, the numbers are absolutely staggering.

It takes a big God to pull that off, doesn't it? No wonder the psalmist marveled that God is mindful of human beings (Ps. 8). Yet this God, incarnated in Jesus, gave us promises that invite us to dream. He assured us he could do the impossible, and he has proven himself often.

What would you do if Jesus came to you in a vision tomorrow morning, stood at the foot of your bed, and said: "I will make available to you all the resources you need, all the courage you need, and all the power you need. Now dream a great dream that is worthy of me." How would you respond to him? Would you have an answer? Are you in the practice of filling your heart with God-sized hopes? Is there some God-honoring vision that makes your heart beat faster? How can your passions be used for his glory? What would it look like for you to cross the finish line of a dream with eternal significance? Think about it, because the truth is that Jesus *has* come to you and made sweeping promises. And the most common reason that those promises aren't fulfilling godly dreams is that dreamers are afraid to believe them.

How God Births Dreams in His People

God gave us a Bible full of stories of people with God-sized dreams who depended on his power and promises to fulfill them. In most cases, Scripture portrays the dreams of these heroes as God-given; in every case they are at least portrayed as blessed and used powerfully by God. Though we call these biblical characters heroes and role models, they were regular people like the rest of us—desperately insecure, uptight about finances, prone to relational conflict, and at times full of fear. Yet something happened with each one of them, some kind of progression that led them from a great dream to a great reality for the glory of God. We can learn a lot from how God dealt with them.

Abraham

It began with a command. God told Abraham to leave his home and go to . . . a place. Not a specific place, as far as Abraham knew. Just an unknown, unnamed place that God would disclose later. As with many dreams, the first step involved getting out of a comfort zone.

Abraham could have pushed that voice aside. We don't know how audibly God spoke to him, but we do know that even though Abraham couldn't see the big picture at first, he believed there was one. Only after he moved out of his comfort zone did God birth a dream in him. He would have descendants whose number rivaled the stars in the sky and the sand by the sea. His family would become a great nation.

The principle we can learn from Abraham is that God often does not birth dreams in us until we've demonstrated that we'll step out of our comfort zone. So the question we need to ask ourselves is whether we're willing to do that—relationally, geographically, financially, or however he leads. To dream big dreams we need to know where our security is. If we find security in the people we already know, the place we already live, or the position we've already grown comfortable in, we may never realize our dream. In fact, we probably won't.

PRINCIPLE
God commands us to step out of our comfort zone.

Joseph

With one of Abraham's great grandsons, God demonstrated that he sometimes puts a dream directly in a person's heart. Joseph had a dream—literally—that he wasn't looking for. He was given two pictures of the rest of his family serving him one day in the future: his brothers' sheaves of grain bowed down to Joseph's sheaf; and the sun, moon, and eleven stars bowed down to him. They were bold, offensive dreams, and Joseph believed they came from God.

If you're like Joseph—and most other people, for that matter—you've found some dreams in your heart that you weren't looking for. You have passions you never even verbalize because they sound so outlandish, crazy, wonderful, and over the top. As God demonstrated with Joseph, however, you can't assume that an outlandish dream isn't from God. Joseph was first a shepherd, then a slave, then the manager of Potiphar's household, and then a prisoner. But God brought Joseph out of prison to fulfill his outlandish dream, and he became the second-highest leader in Egypt and was used by God to prepare for the upcoming famine, thereby saving an entire nation as well as his own family.

PRINCIPLE
God puts his dream in your heart.

Moses

Moses had a dream of seeing his people liberated from captivity in Egypt, but he failed when he tried to accomplish his dream in his own power and according to his own ways. He stepped out of God's path and killed an Egyptian guard—an act that resulted in his having to flee Egypt, not in his people being able to exit Egypt in victory. As Moses lived in exile for forty years, he had plenty of time to reflect on the futility of human effort.

But just because Moses tried to accomplish his dream in human wisdom and strength doesn't mean God didn't put the dream there to begin with. Moses sought the freedom of his people because it was God's appointed time to raise up a deliverer. Moses's failure only served to prepare him to deliver the Jews from Egypt in God's way. He learned the essential lesson that a God-sized dream is impossible unless God supernaturally accomplishes it. (He learned the lesson so well, in fact, that he argued with God at the burning bush about the difficulty of the task.) The result was a deliverer who knew how to rely on the power of God to do things as amazing as parting the Red Sea and providing food in a barren wilderness. God allowed Moses to experience human futility to prepare him for divine success.

PRINCIPLE
God allows us to fail in our attempts to accomplish his dream in our own power.

David

David had a dream—lots of them, in fact. One was to become king and lead well, a dream imparted to him when God told Samuel to anoint David as King Saul's successor. But David spent most of the next decade dodging Saul's spears and hiding in Israel's caves. He faced constant adversity, but he learned during that time to love and trust the God who had called him and promised him royalty. David demonstrated repeatedly that he wanted to please God more than he wanted his dream fulfilled, twice passing up an opportunity to kill Saul and assume the throne.

As a result, we have numerous psalms that give glory and honor to God above all else. Looking back at David, Paul identified him as "a man after [God's] own heart" (Acts 13:22). On what basis is he deemed a man after God's heart? Look at the end of the verse; it is because "he will do everything I want him to do."

Through all the adversity, David learned that his life was not about fulfilling a dream or even about success for God. It's about loving the dream-giver more than the dream. He set his heart on the relationship first and the benefits second. For me, Psalm 73:25–26 has epitomized keeping my love for God ahead of my passion to be used by him.

> Whom have I in heaven but you?
>   And earth has nothing I desire besides you.
> My flesh and my heart may fail,
>   but God is the strength of my heart
>   and my portion forever.

Then note what matters most to the psalmist in verse 28: "As for me, it is good to be near God."

PRINCIPLE

> God teaches us through adversity to love
> the dream-giver more than the dream.

Paul

Paul the Pharisee was a murderer in zealous pursuit of "heretics." What he thought was his greatest service to God turned out to be his greatest failure in life. But God brought him to a

moment of crisis, confronting him with the Savior he persecuted. And in that moment of crisis, God spoke. He gave Paul
a huge assignment that turned into a passionate dream.

God often gives or clarifies a calling during a moment of
crisis. Regardless of the kind of crisis (health, financial, career,
geographical, relational, etc.), we hear him most clearly when
we are desperate for him to speak. When our life is suddenly
in disarray, perhaps even through our own failures, God has a
platform from which to speak. He brings us to a point where
we have to pay attention.

If you're thinking, "Sure, God does that with other people,
godly people who have it together and study their Bible all the
time. But I've been divorced twice, I'm hooked on. . . ." You
can fill in the rest with your own issues, whatever they are.
The point is that even if your issues are as serious as murder,
you're not disqualified. Paul was a murderer, yet God used him
as a powerful missionary.

Remember what God is doing: He wants to accomplish impossible things through improbable people and to impart exceeding
grace to undeserving recipients. My wife, Theresa, found herself
feeling like an improbable person to display God's glory when
she was abandoned by her first husband and left to take care of
two small children. Life can seem completely shattered and futile
at times like that. But God often begins to fulfill dreams at the
point we feel most hopeless about them because that's where his
power and grace can be most clearly seen. Your failures, difficulties, pain, brokenness, hurt—whatever you've been through—are
likely to be the very platform God uses to fulfill the dream he
gave you. God used Theresa's crisis to help others. Because of
what she had been through, he could use her to teach and give
hope to other single moms, helping transform their tattered self-
image into their true identity as daughters of God.

PRINCIPLE
God clarifies our calling in times of crisis
and often uses our worst failures as
the platform of his future fulfillment.

A Big, Hairy, Audacious Dream

I remember a time in 1996 when life began to get really complicated. The church I pastored in Santa Cruz was growing, we were doing five services with video overflow for each one, about six and a half thousand people were coming through our church every seven days, and we had a building on about seven acres with no room to grow. Then an opportunity came up unexpectedly for us to do a radio program, and we began with two or three stations. People began asking us to expand the broadcast and put the message into print as well. All of a sudden, both time and space were rare commodities, and I was overwhelmed.

I met with the elders and told them I didn't know what to do. I had too many opportunities and responsibilities, and all of them seemed to be the right thing to do. I needed God to show me how my life fit with his purposes.

A turning point came at a retreat where we as a staff discussed *Built to Last*, by Jim Collins,[1] author of the original *Good to Great*. Collins wrote that companies with lasting power had "big, hairy, audacious goals." We figured that great goals could happen by human effort, but only God could fulfill God-sized dreams. So we had every staff member take some time alone to do some "sanctified dreaming" and come up with his or her own big, hairy, audacious dream—something only God could do and that could not be defined as the product of human energy or effort.

Our missions pastor, for example, came up with a dream that our church give a million dollars to missions in one of the next three years. At the time, our annual missions contributions were less than half that amount. But in two and a half years, we were able to give over a million dollars. It never would have happened if no one had a dream of doing it. But when people or churches start dreaming, they start gravitating toward those dreams and their priorities and expectations get realigned.

My big, hairy, audacious dream was a little less specific. It came to me while I was sitting out in a field at the retreat. Usually God speaks to me the way he speaks to most people: logical deductions and learned principles that come through Bible reading and prayer. But on this issue of the radio program and the expanding weight of ministry, I asked God to show me how my life fit together. I told him I would do whatever he wanted, but I pleaded with him to give me a less scattered focus.

As I sat in this grassy field, prayed, and waited quietly, I sensed the Spirit of God say very clearly, "Chip, I want you to be a catalyst to transform how Americans think about God, how pastors think about preaching, how churches think about their communities, and how everyday believers live out their faith at home and at work." It wasn't an audible voice, but it was just as clear and very tangible; and I had a strong sense that it wasn't just a suggestion but rather a firm directive. In fact, I vividly heard God say to me, "Chip, write that down. Did I go too fast? Write it down." It was one of the most unusual and powerful encounters I've had with God.

A catalyst is usually a very small quantity of one chemical that, when put into another compound, has a transforming effect on the entire amount. Being a catalyst carries no pressure to be a famous big shot or to be a loud voice. It means simply having a forum that could become one point of influence, the beginning of a chain reaction to help people have a higher view of God and Scripture, to help pastors teach through the Bible with relevance and application, to help churches stop trying to be the biggest one around and instead team with other churches to reach their community, and to help ordinary believers quit living one way on Sundays and another on weekdays. "You asked for a vision, and this is it," the Lord seemed to say. "That's how it fits together. Go do it."

That vision became the rudder of my life since 1996. When Walk Thru the Bible inquired about my becoming their leader, I realized that parts of my vision could not be fulfilled in one location on the coast of California. I could have a radio program and write books from there, but to have a ministry among pastors and churches required connecting with a broader ministry. Walk Thru the Bible had a ministry to forty thousand churches in the U.S. and supplied teaching resources in eighty-five countries. It lined up perfectly.

Like Joseph, I realized God had put a dream in my heart for the purposes he had planned for me. But like Abraham, I really had to step out of my comfort zone. I was at home in California. I lived next to the beach, loved Santa Cruz Bible Church, and had no plans to uproot my family and move across the country. But I had to ask whether I was here in this world for me or for God, for now or for eternity, for preaching to people or for actually living the truth that I preach.

God took my prayer for a dream quite seriously—even more seriously than I did. I came back from the grassy field and told the staff, almost apologetically, about my big, hairy, audacious dream to become a catalyst for transformation. It was an outlandish dream when your church has a radio program on two stations and mentors a few churches. But the staff didn't laugh at me, and five years later we were on about six hundred stations. Only God could do that.

Even though God accomplishes big goals, he usually only does it through people who have made a decision about a dream he's placed in their heart. It's not human nature to move out of our comfort zones and toward long-term impact unless there's a dream propelling us in that direction.

Most of us have small dreams, not audacious ones. We want to buy a second house or be financially secure or play golf for the last ten years of our life. Small dreams of this sort affect a handful of people here and there, and usually only for a brief period of time. One day, when we see the kind of dreams we *could* have had, we'll see these small dreams as missed opportunities.

Can you imagine standing before Jesus one day and saying, "Lord, thank you for preparing me with experience, teaching me with your Word, and giving me all your resources so I could get my handicap from a fifteen to a five"? God would say, "Don't you understand? I prepared you for the most significant season of your life, and you were not on the same page with me. Life is not about you. I have eternal purposes for you, and I'm in the business of doing the impossible through the improbable to impart exceeding grace to undeserving recipients. I positioned you for a great, eternal task, and you missed it."

The Lord is never going to say that to someone who has dreamed great dreams that are birthed through fellowship with him. If you don't have a dream, ask him for one. It isn't complicated, and he delights in the request.

The Dream Will Cost Your Life

Imagine how futile and ridiculous the ministry of Jesus looked as he hung on the cross—a preacher who didn't exactly find success; a miracle worker who suddenly couldn't work a miracle; a loser of epic proportions. But Jesus had said that unless a grain of wheat falls into the earth and dies, it remains only a single seed. If it dies, however, it brings forth much fruit (John 12:24). The dream, it seems, will cost us our life.

This is one reason that most of us don't want God's dream. The dream will cost us our life and appear to others as the height of folly just before God accomplishes the impossible through us. There will be a time in the process of God fulfilling his dream placed in your heart when he will take you all the way to the edge, and you must die.

Every dream passes through the cross. Every dream takes you to where you let go of everything and everyone, every agenda and expectation, and then it is only as the Lord resurrects you and your dream that you can go on.

We spend much of our time and energy trying to avoid that place. We want just enough of Jesus to make us happy, just enough to give us peace, and just enough to make things go our way to fulfill our dreams and our agenda. Meanwhile, he wants to take us to the cross, where our own selfish dreams, egos, and plans for "great accomplishments" have to die. The cross brings you to a place of total and absolute surrender of all you have and all you are. You submit everything in obedience to the vision or dream God has given you for your life.

Scripture and history are replete with examples: Martin Luther and other early Reformers refused to recant their convictions even when their lives were at stake. In the early days of modern missions, missionaries packed their belongings in a coffin because the likelihood of returning to their homeland alive was very slim. Dietrich Bonhoeffer, who stood for truth (and died for it) in Nazi Germany, said that "when God calls a man, he bids him come and die."[2] Embracing God-given dreams means sacrificing the self-inspired dreams, and that's usually a painful exchange. But the benefits always outweigh the costs.

There can be no resurrection without death. It isn't fun, but it's necessary. If you don't die to yourself, then you'll operate out of your natural talents and gifts, and you'll gladly receive the praise for being smart, savvy, and hyperspiritual. That's not the goal. The goal is that God be glorified in your life by doing something impossible through someone improbable like you.

How to Develop Dreams

A very compassionate church member came to me once with a concern. "I have a thirty-three-year-old daughter who has Down syndrome, and we've been in a number of churches over the years. No one seems to care about her. She sits next to me, and I know she makes funny noises, but she really loves Jesus and she wants to grow."

That's a problem I really wanted to solve, but we didn't have anyone who could do that. So I gave her my usual answer as nicely as I could possibly give it. "Dream a dream, form a team, one-page paper." Our church leadership's standing policy was that we were equippers, not hired professionals who did the work of ministry on the church's behalf. So when anyone in our congregation came to us with a desire or burden God had laid on their heart, we told them to prayerfully find others with the same passion and write a one-page summary of how their team might do something about it.

Before long, this woman, who was not gifted as a leader or an administrator, had found two other ladies with those gifts and a heart for special needs, and together they started ministering in that area. Soon we had about sixty Down syndrome and mentally challenged people filling our front section, and a year or two later we were baptizing a lot of them. People knew they could come to our church to receive that kind of ministry.

We didn't have to tell them about a program in Los Angeles or Dallas or anywhere else where they could have their needs met. Someone dreamed a dream and formed a team, and God raised the ministry up.

I know of a missionary in Lima, Peru, who saw the plight of street children—orphaned or abandoned kids who grow up fending for themselves—and began meeting the needs of a few of them. Her mission agency got behind her work, and before long it had expanded into a powerful and fruitful ministry that has become a model for many other cities around the world. The compassion of one woman's heart developed into a mighty tool in the kingdom of God, all because she dreamed a dream and put feet to it.

No dream is too huge for God. Many of them, however, are too huge for us—at least at first. We have to cultivate the art of dreaming, which, as with the lady in our church and the missionary in Peru, sometimes means starting with nothing more than a heart of compassion and an idea to meet a need. Fulfillment often begins with small steps. I believe God often starts with bite-size dreams in specific areas of our life. We begin to express our desires to him, and he takes some of them and puts them together into something he can fulfill.

I've come up with some desires over the years and I generally put them into two categories: personal and ministry-oriented. Not all of them are enormous, though some certainly are. Most are smaller steps in a larger journey. I have found it very helpful to actually write down some of my personal and ministry dreams on three-by-five cards and read them over regularly. Let me give you some examples that might help you in developing your own dreams.

Finish well:
I long to walk with God in the integrity of my heart until the day I die.

One of my dreams is to finish well, to walk with God in the integrity of my heart until the day I die. I can review my progress regularly because I have it written down on a card that reminds me to keep pressing toward that goal.

Worship:
I long to be a true worshiper.

Another dream is to be a true worshiper—to be less self-focused, to enjoy God more, and to sing of his greatness and ascribe worth and praise to him.

Marriage:
I want to love Theresa sacrificially.

With regard to marriage, I wrote down a dream to love Theresa sacrificially in a way that makes sense to her every day. For twenty years I've been reading that over and over and asking God to help me with it. I've also dreamed of praying seriously with her at least once a week, and briefly at least once each day.

Parenting:
I want to help my kids discover the will of God for their lives.

As my kids were growing up, my dreams were to help them discover the will of God for their lives and to help them function in that capacity, to help them identify their spiritual gifts and develop them, and to see them hunger and thirst for righteousness and to know deep in their hearts how loved and significant they are in Christ.

Ministry:

I want to see numerical growth without sacrificing spiritual intimacy and accountability among members of the congregation.

My dreams for ministry have taken different shapes at different times. Back in 1982, I led a church of 35 people in a town of 4,500. I found a card I had written after being there a year: to see numerical growth of over a thousand people without sacrificing spiritual intimacy and accountability among members of the congregation. That may sound preposterous, but I figured God was going to build a great church in a small town somewhere, right? And I was as improbable as the next guy for God to choose for that impossibility. Though my vision of a thousand didn't materialize, the church grew from 35 to about 500, and then God sent me elsewhere. I don't think that kind of growth would have occurred without an audacious dream fueling this small-town pastor.

Preaching:

I long to preach messages that will transform lives for the glory of God.

I also had a dream of preaching great messages that would transform lives for the glory of God. Sounds a little arrogant, doesn't it? But what's the alternative? Would it be better to have a dream of preaching bad or mediocre messages? There's nothing wrong with dreaming about accomplishing great things, as long as that desire isn't focused on one's own glory. To dream of doing great things for God's glory is a biblical goal, and being able to articulate the result we want to see keeps us focused on our priorities and helps us persevere through obstacles and difficulties.

Many of the examples I've listed are small steps to a larger lifelong vision, and you can probably come up with quite a few of your own that will move you closer to your goals as well. Dividing a vision into bite-size portions helps us avoid pie-in-the-sky pursuits—dreams that are so undefined that we can never reach them.

The Process—Getting Started on Dreaming Great Dreams

Practically, what is the process for pursuing a great dream?

- *Write it down.* I find it helpful first to put it down on paper. Write an audacious dream for one area of your life (marriage, children, career, ministry, etc.) on an index card and then develop several smaller steps that will lead you in the direction of that dream. Then do the same for each of the other areas of life. You don't have to show them to anyone; I kept mine private for years because many of them sounded so bold and unrealistic. But to put them down on paper is like making a contract with yourself to move in the right direction.
- *Read them over regularly.* Once you've written down your dreams, read them over regularly. If you constantly remind yourself that you want to be a CEO whose integrity influences your work environment and draws people to Christ, for example, or a mother whose children have a heart for

God because of how you've mothered them, you'll have a hard time getting sidetracked for very long. Reading your dreams again and again will always bring you back to your focus.

- *Pray over them*. Then pray over your dreams. If God is their originator, they will be impossible to fulfill on your own. As you read them, you will be reminded of your utter dependence on him, and you will feel the need to pray for his power to accomplish them.
- *Watch for God's intervention*. Finally, watch for God's intervention and direction. He is your biggest supporter, and he wants to see your dreams fulfilled even more than you do. As long as they are birthed out of your fellowship with him, they are his business as well as yours. You can expect him to work them out in his way and in his timing.

God invites you to dream great dreams, to know him, and to make him known through your personality, passions, gifts, and experiences. He wants to do in you not something good, not even something great, but something impossible.

Action Steps

1. Spend some time this week praying about what you want to accomplish in life. Ask God what dreams he has for you. Remove all restraints and ignore any thoughts of how others might react to your dreams, of resources you lack, or of anything else that would limit you. Let God's Spirit fill your heart with deep longings.
2. Write on four index cards one sentence that expresses your ultimate, lifelong dream in each of these four categories:
   - personal growth
   - singleness, marriage, or family

- professional career
- church and ministry

Then on the back of each of the cards, list the next three steps you believe you need to take to fulfill your dream. Then consider which steps you can take immediately. You want to be sensitive to God's timing, of course, but many people put off their dreams indefinitely because, for whatever reason, they don't feel ready for them. Don't do that. Ask God to lead you decisively in the direction of your dreams this week.

3. Memorize one or both of the following verses:

> You have made the heavens and the earth by Your great power and by Your outstretched arm! Nothing is too difficult for You.
>
> Jeremiah 32:17 NASB

> Now to Him who is able to do far more abundantly beyond all that we ask or think, according to the power that works within us, to Him be the glory in the church and in Christ Jesus to all generations forever and ever.
>
> Ephesians 3:20–21 NASB

Questions for Reflection and Discussion

1. Have you ever been told or taught that Christians aren't supposed to seek the fulfillment of their dreams? Under what conditions is this statement true? When is it false?
2. How can you tell the difference between a self-inspired dream and a God-given one? What would happen to each kind if you brought it to the cross?
3. What God-sized dreams are currently on your heart? Is there any step of faith you could take right now to move toward the fulfillment of that dream? What is it? What is keeping you from taking that step?

5

Pray Great Prayers

Walt Baker made sure he never felt disconnected from Haiti. He had spent twenty years there as a career missionary before he was invited to teach missions at Dallas Seminary, and he had only one nonnegotiable condition under which he would accept that role: he had to be allowed to spend all of every summer where his heart was invested. So each year, Walt gave a group of students an on-the-field education in one of the poorest countries on earth.

I went on a trip to Haiti with Walt and a few pastors and lay leaders in 1982. After a journey that included a plane, jeeps, chicken-infested buses, and donkeys, we ended up at a medical orphanage in a jungle compound. Abandoned children needing medical attention occupied the many cribs in this "hospital of pain." Like the vast majority of Haitians, these kids were in a desperate situation. I had never seen such poverty, and I never have since.

Walt and I shared an area of a house where a couple of cots had been set up. The first night, he asked if I'd like to join him in prayer before we went to bed. We knelt down next to a small desk, and he asked if I would start. I thought we were going to have a nice good-night prayer, so I very sincerely thanked the Lord for the day and asked him to help the orphans.

After a long silence, Walt put his huge paw on my shoulder and began to pour out his heart for Haiti. He talked with God with such passion that I began to feel that my prayer didn't actually qualify as the real thing. I realized that I was in the room with a man who knew God at a level I had never experienced. At times there was a deep sense of reverence and long silent pauses, some of which made me very uncomfortable. Walt talked to God with a sense of authority, as though he actually expected God to do what he asked. He laid the needs out on the table, acknowledged God's unlimited resources, and appealed to the promises God had made. Walt had been surrounded by dreadful poverty for the better part of three decades, returning to Haiti each summer after twenty years on the field. He knew he was praying to a God with power.

Witnessing Walt's fellowship with God made it obvious to me why God used his life. He had a secret weapon of power. I don't know how it happened, but something changed in my heart that night. I told God that I wanted to know him with the degree of intimacy that Walt did. I didn't want to pretend to be like Walt or to imitate his prayers; I wanted the real thing.

We've talked about thinking great thoughts and dreaming great dreams, but praying great prayers moves us onto holier ground. We have a sacred invitation to bring our thoughts and dreams into the presence of God. Jesus articulated that invitation in John 16:23–24: "In that day you will no longer ask me anything. I tell you the truth, my Father will give you whatever you ask in my name. Until now you have not asked for anything in my name. Ask and you will receive, and your joy will be complete."

Imagine if we believed that promise even to a small degree. Receiving whatever we ask in his name—based on his merit and on our relationship with him—is an amazing offer. It's as if Jesus gives us a spiritual credit card with his name on it, and that card is always recognized at the Father's storehouse, where there's unlimited supply. We have to use the card responsibly, of course. Our charges should fit with his purposes. But the conditions are minor considering the scope of the promise.

Jesus gives us an open invitation—he even implores us—to pray great prayers.

Great Prayers Are Deeply Personal

This chapter is not a systematic approach to prayer. It's one man's opinion based on walking with God for over thirty years and being around people whose prayers are powerfully answered by God. Great prayers seem to be accompanied by certain common characteristics.

One of the most noticeable characteristics is that great prayers are deeply personal. They flow from a passion to know God. When a believer is intensely in love with the Lord, his or her prayers begin with him and end with him. Instead of being formulaic, routine, perfunctory, or performance based, great prayers are intimate and heartfelt.

Moses prayed a great prayer in Exodus 33:17–19. The Israelites were camped at the base of Mount Sinai, where God had given the law (and where the people rebelled by making a golden calf to worship), and God had just told Moses it was time to proceed to the Promised Land. Moses had already seen the burning bush, heard God's voice numerous times, and seen miracle after miracle, so a rich prayer life wasn't exactly foreign to him. But he wanted more. Moses prayed for God's presence to go with them, and God assured him that it would. And then he made an audacious request: he asked God if he could see his glory. All the works of God—the dramatic deliverance from Egypt, the miracles and power—were great, but they were not enough. Moses wanted a deeper experience with God himself.

God had to tell Moses that fully answering that prayer would kill him. The unapproachable light and holiness of God would blow his circuits, and the power would destroy him. But God still answered the prayer to the extent he could, putting Moses in the cleft of a rock, guarding him with his hand, passing by, and letting him experience the manifestation of God's presence. When God passed by, he revealed his attributes of goodness, mercy, and compassion. Moses encountered God more personally because he asked to.

David prayed personal prayers too, and we have many of them recorded in the Psalms. He was a great warrior, an accomplished musician, and the king of Israel. He had everything he wanted in terms of wealth and women. So what did he value most? What was his single greatest desire? "That I may dwell in the house of the LORD all the days of my life, to gaze upon the beauty of the LORD and to seek him in his temple" (Ps. 27:4). David's deepest passion was not to get something from God but to be with God himself.

Paul expressed the same passion. He had an impressive pedigree, an elite education, and a highly respected position. But all of that was "rubbish" compared to "the surpassing greatness of knowing Christ Jesus my Lord, for whose sake I have lost all things. . . . I want to know Christ and the power of his resurrection and the fellowship of sharing in his sufferings" (Phil. 3:8, 10). More than anything the world could offer, Paul wanted to have deep, intimate communion with Jesus.

That lines up perfectly with the will of Jesus for those who would follow him. The night before his crucifixion, he prayed a deeply personal prayer to the Father for his disciples: "Now this is eternal life: that they may know you, the only true God, and Jesus Christ, whom you have sent" (John 17:3). God's number one desire for us is that we *know* him, and Jesus's disciples could see his fellowship with God in the nature of his prayers. They had observed him long enough to know the quality of that relationship, so when they wanted to learn to pray, they asked Jesus to teach them.

Jesus gave them an example to follow. We call it "the Lord's Prayer," and the first words in it set the context for the kind of relationship we're to have with God: "Our Father." Literally, that's *abba*, an extremely familiar term that's similar to our words *daddy* or *papa*. In an era in which Judaism was highly formal and focused on the transcendence of God, that was a radical way to address him. A term of endearment like that would have shocked Jesus's listeners.

Sitting next to a pool in Israel a few years ago, I noticed a couple talking and having a drink together after a swim. Their son, who looked about three years old, played nearby and kept calling to his dad. But Dad was having a conversation with his wife and didn't want to get up. Finally, the boy went over to his father, tugged his swimming shorts, and said, "*Abba, Abba, Abba.*" Dad reached down with one arm and lifted his son up onto his lap. As I observed this father respond to his son's cry, Jesus's instruction to his disciples about prayer came into focus for me.

This father-child familiarity is the kind of relationship Jesus taught in the model prayer. The almighty, transcendent God invites you to come to him with childlike dependency and call him *Abba*. You can know that you are deeply loved, that God has nothing but good will for you, and that nothing will ever come between you and him. That's as personal as it gets.

Great Prayers Are Birthed in Brokenness

Not only are great prayers deeply personal, they are also birthed in brokenness. When we come to God with a sense of bankruptcy, knowing we're in a desperate situation and have no resources to get ourselves out of it, God pays special attention. Brokenness will cause us to pour out our heart to God rather than trying to find the right words or the most persuasive arguments to present to him. It's the helplessness we feel when a huge crisis hits or when we're filled with overwhelming remorse, grief, or confusion. Prayers that flow out of brokenness cry out, "I need you!" They come from people at the end of their rope.

David knew how to be broken before God too. He was a godly man who, in a moment of weakness, committed adultery and murder by taking Bathsheba for himself and arranging for her husband, Uriah, to be isolated on the front lines so the enemy would kill him. When Nathan the prophet confronted him with his sin, David's response was not to get defensive and assert his authority as king. Instead, he responded with overwhelming guilt and despair. In Psalm 51 David confessed his sinfulness and pleaded for restoration. He realized how serious his sin was in the eyes of God. This king, who had almost unlimited resources of livestock at his disposal to sacrifice to God in repentance, could have made an impressive number of burnt offerings and tried to put the whole thing behind him. But David knew that a thousand bulls could never connect him with God as well as his brokenness would. "A broken and contrite heart, O God, you will not despise" (Ps. 51:17), he wrote in his desperation. God promises to meet those who, like David, come to him acknowledging their need.

Nehemiah is another example of someone who prayed in brokenness and desperation. He lived at a pivotal point in Jewish history, after many Jewish exiles had returned from captivity in the Babylonian and Persian empires and had begun trying to restore the city. Nehemiah was the right-hand man of the king of Persia, and he heard a distressing report from some fellow Jews who had come from Jerusalem. The exiles who had returned to the homeland were in trouble; the city walls had been broken down and its gates burned. When Nehemiah heard the news, he broke down. He mourned, fasted, and prayed one of the greatest prayers in all of Scripture. This layman—neither a priest nor a prophet—referred to God by name, by personal pronoun, or by descriptive adjective forty-four times in the space of seven verses (Neh. 1:5–11). He was completely focused on God.

That kind of God-centeredness can only come from a spirit of brokenness. When we feel like we have it all together, we base our prayers on *our* situation and *our* needs. But when we see our own insufficiency in light of the holiness and power of God, we focus on *his* agenda and *his* character. We realize that his attributes are worth relying on and ours are not. We base our prayers on who he is.

Everyone, at some time or another, experiences the desperation of an impossible situation. One that I remember well was in the spring of 2003, not long after moving to Walk Thru the Bible. We were running out of money for Living on the Edge, our radio program, and had about fifteen days of cash left before we'd have to shut it down. I cried out to God—literally and figuratively—in my basement, completely broken and unable to solve the problem. It seemed impossible. I have rarely been more aware of human insufficiency, and I knew I had nothing to depend on except the character of God.

The next month—June, which usually begins the summer drop-off in contributions to ministries—we received the largest financial response we'd ever had in a summer month. Out of the blue, it seemed like, God delivered. We never ran out of money, and we never had to go off the air.

It seems contradictory to say, on the one hand, that great prayers begin as personally as "Our daddy" and, on the other hand, acknowledge the enormous gap between his holiness and our complete spiritual poverty. How do we reconcile these first two characteristics of great prayers? Jesus embraced both of them in the first line of the model prayer. We saw that when he taught his disciples to pray, he began with a very personal term for God. But he didn't stop at "Our Father." This is no ordinary, earthly father. When Jesus addressed him in familiar terms, he proceeded with reverent terms: "Our Father in heaven, hallowed by your name" (Matt. 6:9). On one hand, an awareness of the nearness of God makes prayer deeply personal. On the other hand, an awareness of the absolute holiness of God produces that sense of desperate dependency before him.

When was the last time you came to God with a sense of absolute brokenness? When have you felt helpless to accomplish what you thought to be God's will and knew that you had nothing to depend on but God's character? Great prayers are deeply personal, and they also flow from our real sense of need. But even in our deepest need, they focus on God's agenda more than our own.

Great Prayers Champion God's Agenda

God is delighted when our focus shifts from our own needs in our little world to his agenda for his world. There's nothing wrong with praying for our needs, of course. Jesus taught us to ask for our daily bread and the specifics of life. We can come to God in familiar conversation and practice being aware of his presence throughout the day. Taking even the smallest details to him pleases him. But truly great prayers champion his agenda. People who pray great prayers understand God's will for this world and passionately want to see the rule of his kingdom become a reality in their sphere of influence.

Let's take another look at Moses's prayer life. When Moses was on Mount Sinai receiving the Ten Commandments from God, the people God had just miraculously delivered were at the foot of the mountain making a golden calf to worship. They had already seen the plagues in Egypt, walked through the parted waters of the Red Sea, heard God's voice thundering from the mountain, and seen the smoke from his presence, yet they pressured Aaron to make an idol as a representation of God. Then they built an altar, sacrificed to the calf, and turned themselves over to dancing and debauchery.

God presented Moses with a "plan B." In his anger, he would destroy Israel for its stubborn rebellion and make a great nation out of Moses instead. It would have been a sweet deal for Moses, and if he harbored any hint of a personal agenda, he might have jumped on it. But Moses pleaded with God not to implement plan B for two reasons: (1) it would look to the Egyptians like God had brought his people out with the intent to destroy them, and (2) it would break the promise God had given to Abraham, Isaac, and Jacob to make their descendants great. Moses prayed on the basis of his zeal for God's reputation and his awareness of God's promises. There's no indication he even entertained the possibility of becoming the father of a great nation. He championed what he knew to be God's agenda.

Nehemiah did the same thing in his great prayer. After praising God and owning up to the sins of his people, he based his petition on the promise that if God's exiled people returned to him, he would gather them from the farthest horizons and restore them to their land. He reminded God that this was a promise given to *his* servant Moses about *his* people whom *he* had redeemed by *his* strength for the glory of *his* name. He focused the prayer on God's agenda.

There's nothing wrong with reverently but boldly appealing to the promises God has given and the plans he has revealed. Our prayers often ask God to make our life work the way we want it to so we can be upwardly mobile, comfortable, fulfilled, and deeply spiritual without suffering. But *great prayers* seek to blaze a trail for what God wants done in the world more than for what we want done in our lives. Great prayers ask big things of a big God for his glory.

Early in Solomon's reign when he was humble and broken, he asked for wisdom to guide the nation. His prayer reflected his awareness that his kingship was a sacred stewardship over God's chosen people. He asked for discernment between right and wrong so he could guide them as they fulfilled God's will. God was so pleased with Solomon's prayer that he granted not only the wisdom he asked for but also the wealth, victory, and long life he could have asked for but didn't. Because Solomon's prayer championed God's agenda, God's heart was moved.

The first request in the model prayer Jesus taught his disciples also focuses on God's agenda: "Your kingdom come, your will be done on earth as it is in heaven" (Matt. 6:10). It's all about the big picture, and God uses this kind of prayer to direct the course of history. And he's looking for ordinary people like you and me to seek his face and champion his agenda in this hurting world.

Great Prayers Take God Seriously

People who pray great prayers actually think God means what he says. Their prayers are promise centered, not problem centered. Because God is sovereign, omniscient, always good, and unable to lie, when he says he'll do something, he will. Great prayers take the person, the program, and the promises of God seriously.

We start out praying for serious issues—a wayward child, a financial crisis, a failing marriage—with an attitude of faith. But over time, our natural tendency is to turn our prayers into a worry session in which we tell God how upsetting the situation is, how frustrated we are with his delays, and which details he needs to take care of to relieve our anxiety. We even remind him of how faithful we've been to go to church, tithe, and read the Bible—and how punching all those buttons should keep us from experiencing the trial we're in. We end up completely absorbed in our problems rather than focused on his promises.

When we look at God through our problems, the problems seem to get bigger and he seems to get smaller. But when we look at him through his promises, our faith grows and we begin to see him respond to it. That doesn't mean life suddenly becomes easy; he never offered us a life without suffering. In fact, his Word assures us that in the world we will have tribulation (John 16:33) and that all who desire to live a godly life will be persecuted (2 Tim. 3:12). But consider some of the ways we talk ourselves out of believing the truth by focusing on the size of our problem rather than the power of his promise:

"We aren't going to have enough to support ourselves."	"My God will supply all your needs according to his riches in glory" (Phil. 4:19 NASB).
"I'm so overwhelmed with all that's happening; I'm not sure how long I can hang on."	"[God's] grace is sufficient for you, for power is perfected in weakness" (2 Cor. 12:9 NASB).
"I know that's what God wants me to do, but I just can't. It's too hard."	"I can do all things through [Christ] who strengthens me" (Phil. 4:13).
"I don't want to go through this alone."	"I am with you always" (Matt. 28:20).
"I'll never be able to forgive her for what she did."	"If you forgive others for their transgressions, your heavenly Father will also forgive you" (Matt. 6:14 NASB).

This last one is a promise with a condition that's extremely relevant to our prayer life. One of the greatest roadblocks to prayer is unforgiveness. Jesus taught his disciples to ask the Father to forgive them *as they forgave others* (Matt. 6:12). The word he used for *forgive* (*aphiēmi*) literally means "to lay aside," "to send away," or "to yield up." When God forgives us, he doesn't charge our account with the things we've done wrong. He lays them aside and sends them away. But this promise of God's forgiveness is linked to the condition of our forgiveness of others. As we lay aside our claims on other people for their offenses, God does the same for us.

Try this experiment: When you think of the need to forgive those who have trespassed against you, who comes to your mind first? If you heard that this person experienced some kind of misfortune—nothing too serious, but one of life's typical bad breaks—would you secretly feel a little joyful? If the ex-spouse who walked out on you was in trouble, would you have a sense of satisfaction? If the boss who ruined your career or the business partner who robbed you rose to a high level of success, would you harbor some angry fantasies? Most of us would never admit those feelings, but if we're completely honest with ourselves, we can't deny having them—or at least being tempted to have them—from time to time.

People who really believe God's Word take promises like this one—and the conditions that go with it—seriously. That means that if there's bitterness in our heart, we have to deal with it. If our horizontal relationships with people aren't right, our vertical relationship with God can't be right. "The one who says he is in the Light and yet hates his brother is in the darkness until now" (1 John 2:9 NASB). In order to pray great prayers, we have to believe God's promises on the terms with which he offers them. That means asking God to do for others (be merciful and forgiving) what we want him to do for us. We forgive because we have been forgiven.

Those who prayed great prayers in Scripture kept coming back to God's faithfulness to his own words. Again and again, Moses reminded the Lord of what he had promised to the patriarchs: "Remember your servants Abraham, Isaac and Israel, to whom you swore by your own self: 'I will make your descendants as numerous as the stars in the sky and I will give your descendants all this land I promised them, and it will be their inheritance forever'" (Exod. 32:13; see also Deut. 9:27).

Nehemiah reached back into Deuteronomy and reminded God of his promises to Moses:

> Remember the instruction you gave your servant Moses, saying, "If you are unfaithful, I will scatter you among the nations, but if you return to me and obey my commands, then even if your exiled people are at the farthest horizon, I will gather them from there and bring them to the place I have chosen as a dwelling for my Name."

Nehemiah 1:8–9

David reached back to Moses too, appealing in Psalm 103 to the attributes God named for himself when he showed Moses his glory: "compassionate and gracious, slow to anger, abounding in love" (v. 8). David took that description seriously and declared that God removes our sin from us as far as the east is from the west (v. 12). When David's life ended, he wasn't known primarily as an adulterer and murderer; he was known as "a man after [God's] own heart" (Acts 13:22). He wouldn't buy the line many of us use—"I just can't forgive myself"—because the God of the universe had blotted out his sin. People who pray great prayers refuse to live with the baggage of the past because they know that when God says he forgives, it's true.

Paul reflected that kind of confidence in every one of his letters. When he described his prayers for the Philippians, he was certain that "he who began a good work in you will carry it on to completion until the day of Christ Jesus" (Phil. 1:6). For the Colossians, his prayer was that they might know God's will so they could please him with a blameless lifestyle (Col. 1:9–10). He prayed that the Ephesians would know the hope of God's calling, the riches of his inheritance, and the greatness of his power (Eph. 1:18–19). When Paul prayed for the churches he had helped start, he banked on the truth of God's promises and the reality of what God had done. He prayed these truths into Christians' lives because he took God's Word very seriously.

Those who take God and his Word seriously see him work in serious situations. Great prayers aren't characterized by wishful thinking or simply emotional moments with God. Great prayers bring our biggest needs and most difficult struggles to a willing and loving God on the basis of his character and his promises. What big need should you bring to him today? What promise do you need to claim?

Great Prayers Demand Great Courage

Great prayers can be dangerous. They boldly insist—in reverence—that God live up to his character. They have the potential to bring great delight to God's heart, but they take us out of our comfort zone because they bring a demand to the all-powerful King. We know we have no right to *demand* anything of God, so it's an awkward concept for us. But our prayers were never about rights in the first place. They're about the God who has revealed his attributes and told us to rely on them. Great prayers require great courage because they boldly insist, in spite of natural reservations, on what God has said about himself.

Abraham demonstrated this kind of boldness when he interceded for Sodom and Gomorrah. The Lord had told Abraham of the wickedness of those two cities and of his plans to destroy them. Certain that there was a handful of righteous people who lived there, Abraham got confrontational with God over the unfairness of sweeping away the righteous with the evil. "Far be it from you to do such a thing—to kill the righteous with the wicked, treating the righteous and the wicked alike. Far be it from you! Will not the Judge of all the earth do right?" (Gen. 18:25). Abraham appealed to God's justice, reminding the Lord that unfairness is not part of his character. He called a time-out and argued that giving righteous people a raw deal wasn't in God's nature.

Can you imagine talking with the King of the universe like this? Abraham had no right to be so blunt with God—not on his own merit. So he based his prayer on God's character and insisted that God live up to it. You may recall that Abraham kept at it tenaciously. "Would you destroy them if forty-five righteous people are there? Forty? Thirty? What about twenty? Or even ten?" After the first petition, Abraham acknowledged that he was "nothing but dust and ashes." But he continued anyway. After the third petition, he asked that the Lord not be angry with him for persisting. But he still pressed the issue. He was very aware that he might be on the edge of offending a holy, omniscient God, but he also knew that a righteous Judge would be righteous. So he kept asking (Gen. 18:26–33). That's what intercessors do, and God honors it. It's a powerful place to pray from.

Have you had any prayers like that lately? The answer often doesn't come quickly; the test of real praying is when you don't see any results and stick with it anyway. You can do that when you know your prayer fits God's character. Because of who he is, you're sure he wants to resolve the conflict in a relationship, start a new ministry through your church, or meet the financial need of a desperate family, so you persevere.

The danger lies not only in boldly persisting before God but also in standing in the gap as an intercessor. Why? Because that position makes you a prime candidate to become the answer to the prayer. At the end of your persistence, God will sometimes answer your prayers without using you as part of the answer. Frequently, however, he says, "The answer to the prayer is you. You go talk to that person. You start the ministry. You empty your account and meet that need." When an issue you're concerned about keeps coming up in your mind, that's a sign that God wants you to pray about it; but it's also often a sign that he wants you to be his agent and get involved. The danger in great prayers is that when you intercede with God on behalf of people, his response is to ask you to intercede with people on behalf of God. That takes guts.

That was the position Esther found herself in. The Jewish people were facing extermination, and Esther was in a position as queen to intervene. To go before the king uninvited was dangerous; she was risking her life. But, as her uncle Mordecai said, "Who knows but that you have come to royal position for such a time as this?" (Esther 4:14). She realized that God had put her in a unique situation to meet the needs of his people.

Esther agreed to be the answer to Jewish prayers with a sacrificial attitude: "If I perish, I perish" (v. 16).

The same thing happened with Nehemiah. He was burdened by Jerusalem's plight and prayed desperately for about four months. He found out there was a reason he had been so burdened for Jerusalem. He was going to be part of the answer. Like Esther, he would have to risk his life in the presence of the king. He courageously asked for leave so he could oversee the rebuilding of Jerusalem's walls (Neh. 2:1–5). And in the case of both Esther and Nehemiah, the course of world history was changed because they courageously prayed and acted according to God's will.

Jesus prayed the ultimate courageous prayer. One night in the Garden of Gethsemane, he wrestled with the fact that he would soon face the worst combination of physical, emotional, and spiritual pain humanity had ever known. Fully God, he knew that he and the Father had decided on this plan from the foundation of the world. Fully man, he dreaded the cost of saving humanity. His plea for "this cup" to pass from him was a plea for a plan B. If there was any other way for the human race to be redeemed, if there was any way for this excruciating sacrifice to bypass him, he wanted it. But even more, he wanted the Father's will to be done. He was willing to be the answer (Matt. 26:39).

Jesus taught his disciples to pray that way: "Your kingdom come, your will be done on earth as it is in heaven" (Matt. 6:10). In many ways, this kind of prayer is exponentially higher than the great thoughts, great dreams, and great people we've discussed. E. M. Bounds, an American pastor in the late 1800s known for his exemplary prayer life and his writings on prayer, said that what the world needed most was people who pray—not people who talk about prayer or explain it, but who actually do it. Whoever will pray from a deeply personal relationship with God, out of a sense of brokenness, taking God and his Word absolutely seriously, has the potential to change the world. When we can stand in the gap and be willing to be the instrument through which God works—even when we're scared to death—ordinary people like us can dramatically impact the course of history.

Great Prayers Always Go Back to Jesus

Great prayers ask the improbable, expect the impossible, and receive the unthinkable. That kind of extravagant enterprise can only be based on the work of Jesus. He's the great High Priest who blazed the trail for us to come boldly before the throne of grace (Heb. 4:14–16). Our standing before God, any power we have to move his heart, is based solely on Jesus and what he has done. The favor God has bestowed on him is greater than any impossibility we can think of. Is it improbable for a ministry to expand into every nation of the world? For a family that has been dysfunctional for fifty years to be healed? For a pagan country to repent and experience a revival? For your gifts to be used to impact your church, your community, and your world? Perhaps by human standards, but nothing is impossible for God, and he delights in his Son. Those who pray on the basis of his Son's favor will see God doing the unthinkable—"abundantly beyond all that we ask or think" (Eph. 3:20 NASB).

Jesus promised that if we persistently ask, seek, and knock, we will receive what we ask, find what we seek, and see doors open (Matt. 7:7–8). As we become a part of what the Father wants to do in this world, we begin to experience his incomparable power.

John Knox lived in Scotland during the Protestant Reformation, when political and religious tensions were particularly high and persecution was rampant. Knox's résumé wasn't very impressive: a young priest, a bodyguard, an unordained Protestant minister, and a prisoner for his beliefs. But he had a huge vision, and God used his life powerfully. Knox was once overheard praying, "Give me Scotland, or I die!" He became instrumental in the transformation of the country's spiritual life, and his prayers were considered the power behind his influence. Mary, Queen of Scots, was said to have remarked that she feared the prayers of John Knox more than an army of ten thousand.

John Hyde prayed the same prayer for India: "Give me souls or I die!" A missionary in the early 1900s, Hyde became so identified with his prayers that those who knew him called him

"Praying Hyde" and a later biographer called him the "apostle of prayer."[1] He spent long hours each day before God, he woke up three or four times a night to pray, and he often lay on his face in intercession for entire nights. He had few of the gifts associated with effective missionaries: he was partially deaf and had trouble learning Indian languages, he did not have an outgoing personality and often seemed withdrawn, and he seemed more interested in Bible study than in street evangelism. But Hyde had the audacity one year to ask God for at least one converted soul a day, and though many of his colleagues considered it an impossible request, by the end of the year he had led four hundred people to Christ. Far from satisfied, Hyde doubled his request the next year—two souls a day. And by the end of that year he had seen more than eight hundred come to Christ. Later, he doubled that request, and he led more than sixteen hundred a year to Christ. John Hyde prayed great prayers, and thousands of Indians were saved through his ministry.

Hudson Taylor learned how to pray great prayers for provision before he went to China. He reasoned that on the mission field he would have no one to depend on but God, and he would need to know how "to move men by prayer alone." His first great effort at this type of prayer involved receiving his salary without reminding his employer, an often forgetful doctor, to pay him. After having given his last coin to a poor man with whom he had shared the gospel, Taylor returned to his home with empty pockets and a perplexed spirit. But late at night, his employer made an unusual return visit to his office—apparently he had forgotten something—and found an unprecedented weekend delivery there, which included a patient's payment on a bill. He stopped off and paid Taylor his salary, filling the aspiring missionary with faith and teaching him a lesson in God's providence that he remembered the rest of his life.

George Müller approached financial provision with the same kind of faith, asking God to meet every material need as he ran orphanages and influenced thousands without ever having more than a few British pounds in his bank account. All of these ordinary people with extraordinary prayers established incredibly fruitful ministries far exceeding their own resources. They believed that God was serious when he promised that impossibilities would become possible. And they courageously staked their lives on that promise.

I have to confess that I don't pray great prayers very often. But I'm on a journey toward praying the way Jesus wants me to pray and understanding prayer at a higher level than I've ever understood it. I believe God wants you on that journey too, and it begins with the pattern he gave his disciples:

> Abba, Father, holy is your name. I want your kingdom, your agenda, to come and your will to be done on earth with the same effectiveness and power that it's done in heaven. I want you to provide for my daily needs, but I'm not going to stop there. I want you to forgive me and do a work in my heart so that I can forgive those who have offended and wounded me in the same way you've forgiven me. And I want your kingdom, your rules, your power, and your glory to be paramount. I want that so badly that if you tap me on the shoulder in spite of my brokenness and say, "The answer to this one is you," then I'll step up to the plate. I believe that in my weakness you'll give me what I need—in your timing and in your way. Today you'll give me what I need today, and tomorrow you'll give me what I need tomorrow, and as you do, your Word, your agenda, and your glory will be fulfilled.

That's the journey we're on, and I'm not sure we ever really graduate. But I've read and heard about some people who are much further along than I am, and I've met some of them, like Walt Baker, who give me a clear picture of what great prayers are like. When we think of praying like Moses, David, Nehemiah, and other biblical heroes who had a powerful prayer life, we can easily get overwhelmed. But all of them were regular people who started where you and I are starting. I'm convinced that if you ask God to help you learn how to pray great prayers, he'll take you on a journey similar to the ones they traveled. And you'll experience him in ways you've never experienced him before.

Action Steps

1. On one side of an index card, describe an impossible situation you've been facing. On the other side, write your request for God to resolve that situation and Jeremiah 32:17: "Sovereign LORD, you have made the heavens and the earth by your great power and outstretched arm. Nothing is too hard for you." Carry the card in your pocket this week, and every time you pray, pull it out to remind yourself of the great prayer you are praying.

2. Choose one of the examples in this chapter from recent history—John Knox, John Hyde, Hudson Taylor, or George Müller—and search the Internet for more information on that person's life. As you become familiar with him, look especially for three elements: the ordinary aspects of his background, the passion and sense of purpose that led to his great risks, and the ways God honored his faith. Then ask God which lesson from this person's life he most wants you to learn from.

3. Memorize John 16:23–24, "In that day you will no longer ask me anything. I tell you the truth, my Father will give you whatever you ask in my name. Until now you have not asked for anything in my name. Ask and you will receive, and your joy will be complete."

Questions for Reflection and Discussion

1. Why do you think many Christians pray tentatively or limit their requests to what seems "realistic"?

2. How bold are your prayers? Have you ever asked God to do the impossible? What was the result?

3. Do the stories of Nehemiah, John Hyde, and the other examples given in this chapter inspire you or intimidate you? Do you think God based his answers on the special qualifications of the person or on the nature of the prayers they prayed?

6

Take Great Risks

I met Tom Randall in 1976. I remember him as a blur on the basketball court. We were both preparing to go overseas on evangelistic basketball teams—he to the Philippines, I to South America. The difference between us was that Tom had led the nation in scoring for the NAIA at Judson College. He was six-four, he could run like a deer, and it seemed like he never got tired.

Tom was from inner-city Detroit. He talked with a funny accent and seemed kind of crazy. He had only been a Christian for a few months before going to the Philippines to share Christ, but he returned a different man. He later passed up the opportunity to try out with the Chicago Bulls so he could respond to God's call to return to the Philippines and build a ministry. To prepare himself financially, he worked in the factories of Detroit, and then he sold all that he had and left. Now almost thirty years later, a mission organization has been established (World Harvest Ministries), orphanages have been built, and tens of thousands of people have responded to the gospel.

The key to Tom's success has nothing to do with theological education or "playing by the rules." Tom is a risk-taker. Whenever he has heard God's voice, he has responded with reckless abandon. I've been in a Jeep with Tom, with a machine gun pointed in my face, listening to him explain that his friend, "the General," would be quite upset if we were unable to get to the village where we were scheduled to play. I've been on the back of a motorcycle with Tom weaving in and out of traffic, wondering if I would survive the experience. I have more Tom Randall stories than you can shake a stick at, and they all have two things in common: risk and faith.

Tom left for the Philippines thirty years ago with a Living Bible, no formal Bible training, a big heart, and a desire to love a needy people who touched him deeply. In one summer, God turned the leading scorer in the nation for NCAA Division II basketball into a risk-taking, sports missionary whose biography would read like the Indiana Jones of Christendom. He's known as a crazy, wild man inflamed with the love of Christ (who, these days, serves as the chaplain for the senior PGA tour). Tom takes great risks, and he has experienced amazing story after amazing story.

Tom's life has raised some important questions for me: Why does God use some people a lot more than others? Why do some people exude the presence of God and have incredible stories of supernatural experiences? And why do some Christians seem to be in a special category while the rest of us live *regular* lives?

I want to suggest that every Christian's life is marked by windows of opportunity that demand a radical step of faith in order to follow Christ and fulfill his purposes for their life. The difference between good and great is not a matter of knowledge or pedigree but of a willingness to take a radical step of faith.

What makes a step of faith radical is that it will always involve significant risk. In nearly every aspect of your relationship with him, the Lord will bring you to the edge of a decision at which point you'll have to decide whether to leap in the direction he's calling you or pull back to a place that seems safe. That was the issue with Jewish believers when the letter of Hebrews was written, and the writer motivated them with the truth that without faith, it's impossible to please God (Heb. 11:6). Where there is no risk, there is no faith.

That means you can be a good, moral person doing what's expected of you—reading your Bible, going to church, being a responsible spouse and parent, serving in your community—but if you're not living by faith, you won't be very pleasing to God. All of those consistent activities are wonderful; keep doing them. You may have risked a lot to arrive at that level of faithfulness. But if you're playing it safe and staying away from the scary edge of faith, you won't ultimately please God by fulfilling his purposes for you. There are windows of opportunity to break through to a new level with regard to your marriage, your career, your finances, a relationship, or anything else in your life, but breakthroughs require risky steps of faith. To live a great Christian life, you have to expect the supernatural from God.

Here's how that works: at a critical point in each aspect of life, you will have a decision to make that pits obedience against comfort or convenience. If it's a financial decision, you may have to choose whether to start tithing or adjust your current standard of living. If it's your marriage, you may have to choose whether to bare your soul in counseling or let old patterns of behavior keep your relationship in a state of mediocrity. If it's your career, you may have to choose whether to step in the direction of the calling that has gripped your heart or stay where you have a better salary and a comfortable routine. And while you usually know which direction God wants you to choose, you also know most people will think you're absolutely crazy for choosing his will. So in addition to your comfort and convenience, you also risk your reputation—at least with some people.

Where there's no risk, there's no faith; where there's no faith, there's no power or joy or intimacy with God.

Sometimes those people who think you're nuts are close to you. They'll say things like, "Why would you take your family so far away? Your kids will never get to see their friends and relatives anymore." Or, "You're ruining your career," or, "If you give all that money to your church, you won't be able to pay your bills." If you're not careful, the negative words of people who don't have the same vision or conviction God has given you will eventually sound louder than his. Just remember that where there's no risk, there's no faith; where there's no faith, there's no power or joy or intimacy with God. There are also no supernatural miracles, no reward, and, ultimately, no pleasing God.

Without faith, you end up with hollow religious activity, moralistic rules, and dead orthodoxy. Many kids grow up in organizations or churches that have great programs and say the right things about God, but over time their religious activity turns into a lot of rules and little or no power. There's no sense that God is moving. People's lives aren't changing. For someone whose early or only exposure to the Christian faith is all religion and no power, there's little motivation to stick with it.

Contrary to popular belief, it's possible to run a church without faith. You can get people together, run effective programs, make sensible decisions about the budget and the mission of the church, teach Sunday school, and preach sermons, all without getting out of your comfort zone and expecting God to do anything supernatural. A lot of churches that are considered great by people are considered hollow by God. They miss the common denominator of all great Christians: radical faith.

How do we live out a life of great risk as ordinary human beings with ordinary fears? Some people have personalities driven to do things like bungee jumping, skydiving, and investing in volatile stocks. But for most of us, risks are scary. When it comes to our safety and security, we can be quite conservative. Though we tend to think the heroes of faith in the Bible were superstars with bold personalities, they usually were just like the rest of us who live life tentatively. They weren't great because they were fearless but because they acted in faith in spite of their fears.

Because our anxiety about the future can keep us from taking important steps of faith, we need to remember the outcome God promises. We can expect things to end well because God assures us that they will. Jeremiah 29:11 says the Lord knows what he has planned for us, "plans to prosper you and not to harm you, plans to give you hope and a future." We have a sovereign God, and he has already told us the end of the story.

Our King returns riding on a white horse, and his kingdom wins the last battle. He's on our side, and nothing can thwart his victory. We'll go through ups and downs, and we'll sometimes win great victories of faith and sometimes stumble and fall. But we can expect a great outcome from our faith because that's what he has promised. If we never lose sight of that, we can step out in radical faith and see God do miraculous works, just like those ordinary people in the Bible who believed in an extraordinary God.

Old Testament Risk-Takers

When God selected a people through whom to bless the nations with salvation, he began with a man named Abram. Abram was faced with a choice between the status quo and a risky adventure, and he chose to follow God's voice. And God didn't start him out slowly, either. His first instruction to Abram was to leave his home, his land, and his extended family and go wherever this invisible God led. Where? God wouldn't say. Not yet. He had to leave first, then his destination would be shown later.

That's a huge step of faith. Abram was probably secure in the status quo. Then, all of a sudden, a God who couldn't be seen spoke an open-ended command, and Abram and his wife packed up all their possessions and set off toward Canaan (Gen. 12:1–5). He believed the intangible promises of God were more real than the visible reality he lived in, and he acted on what he didn't yet see. That's faith, and with Abram—his name changed to Abraham after he believed—it was radical.

Moses was another man called by God to take a risk. His step of faith involved returning to a country he'd been exiled from, walking into a hostile Pharaoh's courts, and demanding the release of a million or so slaves (Exod. 3:1–10). Moses wasn't exactly fearless; he argued with God, trying to convince him to send someone else. He knew that he was wanted in Egypt dead or alive. He didn't want to go back. But God insisted, Moses obeyed, and even though it looked like a suicide mission at first, God honored his promise and Moses's radical step of faith.

David was young and idealistic, but so were hundreds of the soldiers in Israel's army. Many of them probably knew how to use a slingshot as well as David did. Every member of the army, however, looked at Goliath, heard his taunts against God and his people, and only *wished* they could do something about it. No one stepped up to the plate—except David. David was so offended by the giant who slandered Israel's God that he was willing to risk his life (1 Sam. 17:20–37). God was pleased with that risk of faith, and the rest is history.

Esther confronted evil at high levels of authority. We read her story—how this Jewish girl became the queen of Persia and God used her to save the Jews from extermination (Esther 5–7)—and we perhaps don't realize the risk she took. But her life was genuinely on the line. It was easy for the king to get a new wife from his vast harem if the current one did something to offend him. That's what happened to his previous wife; she had a bad day and was gone. So when Esther broke protocol and went into the king's court to tell him about the plot to kill the Jews, she could have been put to death at the king's whim. Was she afraid? Of course—anyone would have been. But she acted in faith, God was pleased, and Jews were saved from the threat of annihilation.

New Testament Risk-Takers

Lest you think all the great people of faith were in the testament in which arks were built, seas parted, walls fell down, and other such dramatics were displayed, the New Testament has no shortage of risk-takers either. Take Peter, for example. Jesus was walking on the beach, saw Peter and Andrew casting their net into the lake, and said, "Follow me . . . and I will make you fishers of men" (Mark 1:16–17). So Peter and his brother dropped their nets and followed him, and we think, "What a nice story," and go on to the next verse. But have you thought about the implications of that decision? I can imagine his father: "You're doing what? I've been building this business for years. How will you support yourself now?" We learn later that Peter was married. Can you imagine his wife's reaction? "You're seriously going to follow an itinerant preacher and be gone for weeks at a time? How will you support our family? What about our future?" Peter left the security of his family and his financial base and confronted his fears, as well as the religious establishment that threatened to cast Jesus's followers out of the synagogue. Does that sound like a radical, risky step? You better believe it.

Paul took a few risks himself. He thought his calling was to kill those heretical Christ-followers, and then he encountered Jesus on the Damascus road (Acts 9:1–6). He had to go to the apostles he had been trying to kill, and if it hadn't been for Barnabas, they wouldn't have even considered seeing him. Later he went to his hometown of Tarsus. As a Roman citizen and a Jew tutored by Gamaliel, the most famous rabbi around, he had enjoyed a certain amount of prestige and privilege. But he returned to the city where people would call him a fool for giving up everything for a teacher executed by the government years before. Once after being dragged out of a city, stoned, and left for dead, Paul regained consciousness, got up, and immediately walked back into the same city (Acts 14:19–20). Why? Because the promise and calling of an invisible God were greater to him than the circumstances that threatened his life. That's radical.

Jairus is another example. He was a ruler in the synagogue who laid his reputation on the line to seek Jesus's help. Even the act of suggesting that Jesus come heal his daughter could have been enough to cause him to lose his position, the benefit of all his years of religious training, and the right to worship at the synagogue. But Jairus's daughter was dying, and he was desperate. He risked everything for a chance at experiencing the power of God (Luke 8:41–42, 49–56).

So did a woman who was hemorrhaging blood. For twelve years she had been bleeding—a condition that made her ritually unclean and therefore unable to worship at the temple, even for required festivals and sacrifices. She violated all kinds of cultural norms and biblical instructions as an unclean person by pressing through a crowd and touching the garment of the

Son of God himself. She was trembling with fear when she did it, especially when Jesus turned around and asked who had touched him. Still, she told him her embarrassing situation in front of a crowd, most of whom would have chastised her and sent her away immediately. But Jesus loved the risk she took. It demonstrated great faith (Luke 8:43–48).

A radical risk-taker is like a poker player who finds himself in a make-or-break moment and pushes all of his chips to the center of the table. He says, "I'm all in," and holds nothing back. Family, finances, reputation, future—anything or everything is at stake in a radical step of faith, and you push your chips to the middle of the table and depend entirely on God. In order to reap a great reward, there has to be a great risk.

Desperate situations and humble attitudes allow us to put everything at stake in spite of our fear. People who take radical steps of faith don't do so because they come to a surreal, godly moment in life when they are confident and superspiritual. God often brings these windows of opportunity when we are most desperate and don't have anywhere else to go. Our ears open up, and we are willing to hear him say: "Go take a new job." "Deal with this marriage issue." "Move to a new city." "Get out of your comfort zone and reach the people I want to reach." "Give your money away." "Face that addiction, even though your reputation is on the line." The situations we think are bad, God can use for good. He brings us to whatever point of humble desperation is necessary to get us to take a step of faith. But those who take radical, risky steps of faith into the places God is leading them are used greatly by God. And those who don't, aren't.

Be careful, though. The dynamic between faith and foolishness can be tricky. Many Christians have done some very misguided or even dangerous things under the guise of faith. Taking great risks must fit with God's clearly revealed will. He is never going to lead you to do something that contradicts his Word, and he expects every "risky" decision we make to be accompanied by wise counsel and much prayer. There's a distinction between radical steps of faith and reckless steps of foolishness. When God has called us to move in a certain direction, a step of faith will get us there. When he hasn't, a step of faith will move us away from his will.

That doesn't mean our risks will always look reasonable to the people around us. The Bible is full of examples of godly people who looked absolutely ridiculous obeying the Lord's instructions. Abraham and Sarah believed God would give them a child in their old age—a belief most of us would consider delusional if we hadn't already read the story (Gen. 18:1–15; 21:1–7). God told Gideon to whittle his army down from thiry-two thousand men to three hundred—an act of faith that the "wise counsel" of godly observers would strongly advise against (Judg. 7:2–8). Paul looked rather foolish when, after being dragged out of town, stoned, and left for dead, he got up and walked back into the same town. Jesus delivered God's people by doing what looked like the opposite of deliverance—submitting to a Roman execution. When we are deciding whether to take a great risk, we have to remember that God often chooses foolish-looking plans in order to shame the wisdom of the world (1 Cor. 1:27). The difference between faith and foolishness isn't the degree of risk. It's God's will. The only way to know that is to immerse yourself in prayer and his Word while seriously considering what he might be saying to you through the counsel of godly, biblically minded people.

Risk Is in the Eye of the Beholder

Risk doesn't look the same to everyone or in every situation. What I think is a radical step may be hardly anything to you, and what you think is a major leap may be easy for me. God may lead some people to get out of an unhealthy relationship and leave it behind. It's not the right place at this time in your life. For others, sticking with a relationship in distress—or returning to face one that broke down long ago—may be the step of faith God is asking for. Risk can take the form of stepping up and fighting, like David did against Goliath; it can mean confronting your own issues or someone else's; or it can even be waiting on God when everything in you wants to move ahead and act on a promise for the future. We have to be very careful about defining a step of faith for someone else.

We also have to be careful not to think faith is a nebulous concept that's always out there but rarely reachable. Radical steps of faith are concrete. They always have at least two things in common: they involve risk, and they fit with God's clearly defined will.

Risk-takers also always have a few things in common. One of them is fear—the emotions you feel that make you want to find a reason not to do what God is calling you to do are normal. We all have them. We fear what might happen. Esther didn't enter the king's court thinking, "Okay, let's get this done because I have a hair appointment at 2:30." She was scared to death. Peter didn't say, "Sure, Jesus, I'll follow you for a little while. No big deal; this could be fun." Fear and faith are not necessarily antithetical.

The greatest steps of faith I've ever taken have all been accompanied by fear—sometimes absolute terror. This is why the most common command in the Bible is, "Do not be afraid," or something like it. Usually when God speaks, whether through an angel or some other dramatic event, the first words are, "Fear not." That's not a condemnation of fear; it's all right to be afraid. But it's not all right to let fear paralyze you and prevent you from taking a step of faith. In the battle between faith and fear in your life, faith needs to win.

History is full of heroes who stepped out in faith even when the odds were against them. Christopher Columbus had a quite good chance of falling off the edge of the earth, according to many of his contemporaries, but he sailed westward anyway. Martin Luther confronted a massive medieval institution when he nailed on a church door his ninety-five theses challenging corruption and unbiblical tradition in the church. Rosa Parks faced the wrath of a deeply ingrained culture when she refused to give up her seat on a bus simply because she was black. Nearly everyone noted for a great "first" faced enormous odds, and we honor them for it. Greatness only comes through obstacles.

Risk-takers step out in spite of their fear, regardless of obstacles and perceived dangers. Those who believe God's promises enough to move forward in spite of the perils all have something in common: they receive the favor of God. That's the encouraging part. God's reward and blessing come into their life. We often quote the first half of Hebrews 11:6: "Without faith it is impossible to please God." That's true. But the second half of the verse is just as important: "Because anyone who comes to him must believe that he exists and that he rewards those who earnestly seek him."

The first half of that truth is that we are to live our lives as though an all-powerful, all-knowing, loving, compassionate God actually exists and cares about us. Many people believe in God but never act as if he really exists. We can't do that and still act in faith. The second half of that truth is that we must believe God really does richly reward those who seek him diligently. He isn't a parent with arms crossed just waiting for us to mess up so he can dole out his punishment. He's encouraging us to jump off the diving board into the water so we can experience how great it feels. He wants us to take that leap so we can know the reward and so he can reveal himself to us in powerful new ways.

When we take a step of faith like that, it pleases the heart of God. I encourage you to read the Gospels with new eyes. Get a cup of coffee sometime and sit down with your Bible. Start in Matthew and read as fast as you can, looking for the words *faith*, *believe*, and *trust*. The four Gospels are the length of a short novel, and you're only looking for these three words, so it shouldn't take too long to get through them. What you'll find is that Jesus has only one agenda. For the most part, the only times he ever gets upset with his disciples, their lack of faith is the issue. His singular agenda is that they trust his character and his Word.

Faith is simply doing what God tells you to do whether you feel like it or not—especially, in fact, when you *don't* feel like it. You obey regardless of the circumstances because he said to and his Word is true. Great risk-takers operate in faith in spite of their fear, and they experience God's favor—not because they're better, smarter, were raised in a better home, know the Bible better, and have no baggage. If those things were required, most of the characters of the Bible would have been disqualified. If you think you come from a dysfunctional family, try reading the stories of Abraham, Isaac, Jacob, and Joseph sometime. And yet these are considered the "fathers of faith." They are described in the Old Testament as far from perfect, but they are installed in the New Testament's "faith hall of fame." Isn't that encouraging? The favor of God comes not to those who have it all together but to those who choose to believe, who act in faith despite their fears.

Where Are You?

As you've been reading this chapter, in what area have you sensed God challenging you to step out in faith? Has the Spirit of God used any of these examples to pull you toward a certain action that is risky and would require you to depend completely on God? Think through your relationships, your work, where you live, how you spend money—in other words, think through the key areas of your life. What has God put his finger on?

With that issue in mind, let me pose another question. If God is, in fact, bringing into each of our lives windows of opportunity to act in faith, and if our life is really determined by our response to these windows of opportunity and the level of risk we're willing to take, how can ordinary people like us become great risk-takers? Some of us, after all, are still eating the same kind of breakfast we ate in 1972. It was good then, always has been, so why change it now? Some of us simply don't like risk.

I hate to break the bad news, but avoiding risk is not an option in the Christian life. God understands that faith can be scary and that our sense of security feels threatened, but he didn't give us any kind of "diet Christianity" with no risks added. There's only one Jesus to follow, and you can't follow him without being willing to take radical steps of faith. So how can we break out of our comfort zone and go for it?

How to Become a Great Risk-Taker for God

The end of Hebrews 10–11 gives us three great answers to that question: refocus your fear, rejuvenate your faith, and recall his faithfulness. When you do these three things, you'll progressively become a great risk-taker.

Refocus Your Fear

The letter to the Hebrews was written to Jews who had embraced Jesus as the Messiah. He had wonderfully changed their lives, they began to walk with him, and things were going very well—for a while. Then persecution came, and the price tag for following Jesus kept getting higher and higher. Many of their friends and family were telling them that they could come back into Judaism, adhere to the laws and teachings of the rabbis, and then quietly add Jesus on the side. That way, they could fly under the radar as a Jew and not be persecuted by the religious authorities.

The writer of Hebrews expresses how God feels about people who want to sink back into religious moralism and hollow rituals as opposed to living by faith. "'My righteous one will live by faith, and if he shrinks back, I will not be pleased with him.' But we are not of those who shrink back and are destroyed, but of those who believe and are saved" (Heb. 10:38–39). Then he explains what faith, having that kind of importance, actually is: "Faith is being sure of what we hope for and certain of what we do not see" (Heb. 11:1).

In other words, faith is operating on the reality that we know to be true, even though we don't see it. When the Bible uses the word *hope*, it isn't expressing the same concept we mean when we use that word. We say that we hope the weather will be nice or that the stock market will go up. That's not hope, that's wishful thinking. *Hope* is fixing our eyes on a promise that's guaranteed to be fulfilled and living in the present in light of that future certainty. So *faith* is being certain of an invisible reality and acting on it.

This, according to the next verse, is what the ancients were commended for. They may or may not have made all the prescribed sacrifices at the right times and in the right ways. None of them were morally perfect or operating out of completely pure motives. They experienced God's favor because of faith—nothing else. And people who pulled back and were unwilling to take a radical step of faith did not please God.

To point out how irrational unbelief is, the writer reminds his readers who it is they're actually supposed to be trusting: "By faith we understand that the universe was formed at God's command, so that what is seen was not made out of what was visible" (Heb. 11:3). An infinite, eternal, self-existing being spoke words of command, and out of nothing came two billion galaxies. In one of them consisting of two billion stars, there's a small solar system. In that solar system, a small planet called Earth was designed to sustain life. And one tiny little dot on that planet is you. The writer of Hebrews points out that the one who spoke all of that into existence is the one who has promised to be with us always. If he says, "This is my Son," we can believe in his Son in spite of persecution. If he says, "Confront this issue in your marriage," we can confront it in confidence. If he says, "I want you to be free from clinging to money and possessions as your security," we can give liberally. Whatever he says to do, whether it's facing temptation, getting rid of an addiction, beginning a new career, moving to a new place, or anything else that seems frightening, we can do it because we know who he is.

So why did I call this point "refocus your fear" instead of "get rid of your fear"? Here's my theory on fear: we're always going to be afraid of something, but I would rather fear God than fear people or circumstances. The reason many of us won't take risks is that we're afraid of losing people, things, or security. When we face one of those windows of opportunity for radical faith, we'll often find that the decision is between doing what God wants and maintaining others' opinion of us. If we try to please God, we won't please them, and if we try to please them, we won't please God. We will seek the favor of whomever we respect and honor (i.e., fear) the most.

That's why Scripture says, "The fear of the LORD is the beginning of wisdom" (Ps. 111:10). The fear of God is a novel concept today, but it is biblical. It leads to wisdom—understanding how God has arranged life, what his priorities are, and how to do relationships, money, and everything else his way.

Billy Graham once took a radical step of faith that illustrates a desire to fear God more than other people. The context was the racial conflict of the 1950s and the beginning of the civil rights movement. Graham's ministry was beginning to grow rapidly, and in the North and West he spoke to integrated audiences. In the South, however, organizers of his crusades always segregated the audience. That was actually a step in the right direction, because in previous decades only white audiences would have been allowed to attend. Key people around Graham acknowledged the need to speak to both whites and blacks in the South, but they said mixing them together would cause him to lose his reputation among those who supported him financially.

At first Graham tried to create a middle ground that opposed both forced integration and forced segregation. But over time, the issue became so intense that he couldn't find any middle ground at all. Reporters asked him again and again why he addressed racism in his messages in the North and West but not in the South. Segregated events had always struck him as wrong, but he had never chosen to take decisive action—until one crusade in Jackson, Mississippi.

The governor of Mississippi had suggested separate meetings for blacks and whites, but Graham wouldn't agree to that. So he preached in a crusade where all whites were on one side, all blacks were on the other, and ropes stretched down the middle aisle keeping the two apart. Just prior to one of his messages, he walked toward the ropes of separation and pulled them down. Mystified ushers awkwardly tried to put them back up, but Graham personally stood in the way. Returning to the stage, he said there was no scriptural basis for segregation and that it had no place in church. It touched his heart, he said, to see whites and blacks standing shoulder to shoulder at the cross. This powerful gesture marked a major ministry watershed; he never again led a crusade with a segregated audience.

We read about Billy Graham and consider him to be a spiritual superstar. I've been privileged to speak at his leadership center several times and have gotten to know people who know him well, and everyone talks about how grounded and genuine this farm boy is today. He's a regular guy with a humble attitude. So why did God use him so mightily? He was willing to take radical steps of faith. He received a tremendous amount of flack for his stance on segregation, as everyone in the civil rights movement did. There were extraordinary risks involved. But at critical windows of opportunity in his life and ministry, God said, "I want you to step out in faith." The moment Graham pulled down those ropes, his whole ministry could have fallen apart. He was in a position of having to fear God or fear man, and he chose to be obedient to God.

Who do you fear? If you're afraid of what other people will think, why? What is it about their opinion that matters so much, and why doesn't God's opinion matter more? The worst that can happen to you by fearing God is offending people. The worst that can happen by fearing people is offending God—and missing out on many of the blessings he wants you to experience.

Rejuvenate Your Faith

The next two verses of Hebrews 11 are interesting:

> By faith Abel offered God a better sacrifice than Cain did. By faith he was commended as a righteous man, when God spoke well of his offerings. And by faith he still speaks, even though he is dead.
>
> By faith Enoch was taken from this life, so that he did not experience death; he could not be found, because God had taken him away. For before he was taken, he was commended as one who pleased God.
>
> Hebrews 11:4–5

After the reminder in verse 3 of who God actually is, the writer gives us two examples of radical faith that aren't usually mentioned along with dramatic stories like the Red Sea or Daniel and the lions' den. The first is about a man who came to God with an offering, and the second is about another who had such a close relationship with God that the Lord just took him up to heaven rather than waiting for him to die. And then comes the well-known verse we've already quoted: "Without faith it is impossible to please God, because anyone who comes to him must believe that he exists and that *he rewards those who earnestly seek him*" (Heb. 11:6, emphasis added).

I believe God inspired the writer of Hebrews to give these two examples first for a reason. If you want to rejuvenate your faith, start with the little things. Abel's offering was a normal act of faithfulness in the area of his income. One of the quickest, easiest ways to rejuvenate your faith is in the area Jesus emphasized most frequently: your finances. He told his disciples that they could worship mammon (money, security, possessions) or they could worship him (Matt. 6:24). There was no middle ground. He also told them that whoever was faithful in a small thing—money—would also be faithful in much (Matt. 25:23). In other words, if people can't trust him with their finances, they're not even up to the plate in the spiritual things. We can say that we love God, go to church, and worship him with tears in our eyes and our hands raised high, but if he doesn't have our treasure, he doesn't have our heart.

Giving back to God the first and the best of what he has given you will remind you that it all belongs to him, which will increase your faith. The minimum is a tithe, but if he has given you a lot, he invites you to test and see how powerful and faithful he is by giving even more. The average evangelical in America gives 2.7 percent of his or her income. Do you know what that says to God? "I know you created the universe, I love Jesus, I believe you can forgive my sin and take me to heaven, and I ask you to provide for all of my family, but I don't think you're big enough to handle my money—I mean the money you've entrusted me with. I don't believe you'll provide for me if I give some of it back to you."

How does God respond to that? "Okay, I accept your decision. You can work out your life with your resources. I don't need your money; that wasn't the point. I wanted your heart and longed to cultivate your faith." One of the quickest and easiest ways to see God work in supernatural ways is to give, then wonder how your needs are going to be met, and then watch him supply. Many Christians have never experienced that, but if you start there, your faith will be rejuvenated. You will begin to see God work in ways you never imagined as you incrementally begin trusting him with more of your money.

The second way to rejuvenate your faith is by pondering the big issues. The story of Enoch has very little information in it, but what's there is fascinating. When Hebrews 11 starts out with these examples of how to really walk with God, my initial reaction is to question why Abel and Enoch are the first two mentioned. Couldn't God have inspired some better stories than Enoch to come up at this point? But if you go back to Genesis and look at the genealogy in which Enoch appears, you discover a deep lesson about how to please God.

The genealogy in Genesis 5 is one of those passages you tend to skim through when you're on a Bible-reading plan. In King James English, it's a bunch of *begat*s. But the *begat*s are interrupted by a couple of comments about Enoch: "After he became the father of Methuselah, Enoch walked with God 300 years and had other sons and daughters. Altogether, Enoch lived 365 years. Enoch walked with God; then he was no more, because God took him away" (Gen. 5:22–24).

You don't find that kind of statement in most family trees, but God wanted to point out something remarkable about Enoch. What was it that made this man so remarkable? Why did God so treasure his relationship with Enoch that rather than let him die, he supernaturally transported him directly to heaven? Here was a normal man doing life, working hard to make a living, experiencing the normal pressures we all face, and sticking with it for a long time. Then something happened in his life that rearranged his priorities and transformed his perspective. He went from just another name who "begat" so-and-so to God's example in Hebrews 11 of one of the greatest men of faith of all time. What happened? What we know primarily about Enoch is that he walked with God. Amid all the pressures of life, Enoch made his relationship with God his priority, and the passage is worded in such a way that seems to indicate his first son's birth was a catalyst for that change in priorities. Enoch apparently held that baby boy in his arms, began to ponder the big things in life, and realized that the biggest things are relationships.

I vividly remember holding my firstborn in my arms minutes after he entered the world; I was crying, overwhelmed with emotion. Life is amazing. People are what really matter. That must be something like what Enoch experienced. And his life so reflected that truth that God didn't wait for him to die to bring him home.

By contrast, I've known countless people in the middle of life who lament having almost no relationship with their parents. Now those parents are sitting in an assisted living facility somewhere, and connecting at this point seems virtually impossible because the relationship has been distant and strained for the last twenty years. Many of those people will be sitting in the same kind of facility years from now because they have so many other priorities right now and are not building relationships with their own spouses and children. When most people finally realize that we're usually only remembered for the people we touched rather than the things we accomplished, it's almost too late to invest in much eternal treasure. Enoch built a life around the big issues—a relationship with God and others—and God was pleased enough to take him from this life.

In order to rejuvenate our faith, we must practice faithfulness in the small things and ponder the big things while we remember the main thing: pleasing God. Without faith, it's impossible to please him.

Unfortunately, many of us try to please him in other ways. The supposed path to his approval is steeped in our culture and ingrained in our thinking. We believe that if we can get our morals straight, get our family in line, get married (if we're single) or have children (if we're childless), find the right kind of work in the right place at the right time, and even serve in the church or go on mission trips, we'll be fulfilled and God will be pleased. We unconsciously have a mental picture of what it would take for life to be "just right." We try to stop doing bad things, start doing good things, and assume the result will be the "abundant life" of personal satisfaction and fulfillment. But the goal of life is to please God, and without faith, that's impossible.

Am I saying all those things are wrong? Absolutely not. Going to church, reading your Bible, praying, having a family, doing meaningful work, and all those other things we do to try to please God are good—with the right motive. If we do them not to earn God's favor but to live out his truth, then they are wonderful. But to actually please him, there has to be faith.

Recall God's Faithfulness

Read the rest of Hebrews 11 sometime (verses 7–40) and it will reinforce God's faithfulness in your mind. You'll see what God did with the faith of those who took great risks. Through Noah, he saved the human race from complete destruction; he gave Abraham his own nation and blessed all other nations through him; he gave Sarah a child when she was ninety years old; he delivered God's people through Moses; he collapsed the walls of Jericho through the obedience of his people to a strange command; he made a hero out of a prostitute; and the list goes on. It doesn't end with Hebrews 11 either. Throughout church history and throughout your life and mine, God keeps bringing windows of opportunity for ordinary people like us to exercise faith in the areas of our families, finances, ministries, work, relationships, and more. And when we do, we get a glimpse of what faith in a faithful God really looks like.

Recalling God's faithfulness is one reason I read his Word every day. I get up in the morning and read it first thing because I need to remember that he has kept all his promises to those who stepped out in faith. Left to myself, I forget that and get awfully scared. So during my quiet time, I often write out all of my fears in my journal—like I did this morning—and then tell the Lord I can't handle them. I willfully give him the circumstances of my life and ask him to show me what it looks like to trust him in each area. "How do you want me to trust you in my ten o'clock meeting?" "What does faith look like in this pressure I'm feeling about my finances?" "How can I depend on you to meet the deadline on this book? I'm overwhelmed and tired!" Then a few days later, I go back and put a little check mark and write the date beside each issue he helped me resolve. I've got stacks and stacks of journals with check marks from the last couple of decades to remind me that what was impossible on a Tuesday was answered on a Thursday or Friday—or even a year or two later. Reviewing those helps build my faith tremendously.

That's especially true when I have a big decision to make. When God called me from Santa Cruz Bible Church to be president at Walk Thru the Bible in Atlanta, my response was, "Lord, please don't make me go! I love the church; I love my wife, who doesn't want to go; I love our security here; and life is really working here. It's wonderful. My kids love it here. Please, please, please let me stay." Somehow, I got from there to, "Okay, I'll go. And I'm sure it will be wonderful."

It wasn't wonderful at all—for the first two years, anyway. My wife went through a horrendous time, there was a dip in the economy, the ministry's resources were strained as a result, and God took me on a journey I would never have chosen to go on myself. Why? Because his agenda is to make me more like his Son and to use my gifts to impact and love other people. When God wants to do something broader through you than he's currently doing, your radical step of faith will often take you into a deeper experience with him. Suffering creates dependency, and pain brings an aspect of purity to your motives that nothing else can. But suffering because of faith always comes with God's promise that he rewards those who diligently seek him.

I came up for air almost four years later, and Theresa and I were recently reflecting on God's goodness and sovereignty in that decision. We recalled how we had been willing to submit to God only after a rather intense struggle. God made it very clear I was to do this, and Theresa didn't want to. I wrestled with that, and so did she. She finally said, "If you really believe it's God's will, I'll trust you and go. Just know that emotionally I don't want to." And as we sat on our deck a few months ago and considered all that had happened, we counted our blessings. Two of our sons relocated with their families to Atlanta. We didn't have any grandchildren when we came, but we've had one each year since moving, with three more on the way. The ministry has greatly multiplied its impact around the world and is in a position to bear more fruit than I ever thought possible. Neither Theresa nor I would ever have chosen this for ourselves up front, but looking back we can see the amazing richness of God's reward and grace. And we would never have experienced that grace in this way if we had not taken a radical step of faith.

Now when I'm faced with a big decision, I can look back at God's grace and faithfulness in that situation—as well as many others I've experienced—as a reminder that he will be there in the scary risks I'm called to take. The character he has demonstrated in the past is true for the future because he never changes. Recalling God's great faithfulness in the past empowers us to trust him for still greater things in the future.

Faith Is a Verb

Great risk-takers see faith as a verb, not as a noun. It isn't what you *have* as much as what you *do*. The kind of faith that prompted Abel to give an acceptable offering, Noah to build an ark under sunny skies, Abraham to leave home, Daniel to pray even under the threat of death, and on and on, is faith that leads to action. It is living out what God has said, knowing it's true because of his character, and knowing that there might be a heavy cost involved. Many of the examples Hebrews 11 lists are people who pleased God but did not yet see the kingdom that was promised. Their faith did not result in the American dream. Some were killed, exiled, or otherwise persecuted, and the world wasn't even worthy of them. But they pressed ahead and took great risks, because that's what faith does.

Great Christians don't play it safe. Where there's no risk, there's no faith. What specific steps of faith do you sense God prompting you to take? Is there something or someone God wants you to leave behind? Something or someone to return to and make things right? to confront? to step up and fight for? Do you need to stop worrying about what people think and do what you know God has called you to do?

I encourage you to prayerfully consider each of those questions. As you read them, a specific situation or two probably popped into your mind. Ask the Lord what he wants you to do in those situations. Write out your fears and ask him what trust looks like in the midst of each one of them. Then, when he has laid out a clear, scriptural response in your heart and mind, act on it in faith—even if it's risky, because God is looking for great Christians, and great Christians take great risks.

Action Steps

1. Think of one great dream or prayer you feel God has laid on your heart. Then draw three columns on a sheet of paper. In the first column, write down the steps you would need to take for your hopes in that area to become a reality. In the second, list any external obstacles (circumstances, people, finances, etc.) that are in the way. In the third, list any internal obstacles you have (fears, doubts, etc.) that might keep you from taking a great risk. Use this paper in your quiet times this week to pray through the issues you face. Ask God to help you discern between faith and foolishness and to help you move in the direction he has called you.

2. Identify someone in your relational network who took a huge risk in a career or family decision. Arrange a time to talk with that person over lunch or coffee and ask a lot of interview-type questions. What fears did he or she have to overcome? How hard was it? How satisfying has it been? What advice would he or she give someone who's praying about a scary decision? Let that person's experience inform, inspire, and encourage you.

3. Memorize Hebrews 11:6, "Without faith it is impossible to please God, because anyone who comes to him must

believe that he exists and that he rewards those who earnestly seek him."

Questions for Reflection and Discussion

1. Think of a situation in your past in which you took a risk.
   What fears did it bring up for you? What aspects of it appealed to you?
2. What reactions would you expect to get from your family and friends if you took a great risk that didn't make
   sense to them? What criteria would you use to distinguish
   between godly counsel and human wisdom?
3. Do you sense God leading you to take a risky step of faith?
   If so, what might be keeping you from taking that step,
   and how can you overcome it?

7

Make Great Sacrifices

Across the table, the pastor of an underground house church in China shared what was going on in his life and how his ministry had been going recently. He had come to Hong Kong for a Walk Thru the Bible training seminar I was leading, and after one of the sessions we went out for dinner. His congregation had to move frequently because government officials in his province were particularly hard on house churches. He told me about his evangelistic trips and how he missed his wife and children whenever he traveled.

While he was away on a recent trip, the police came into his home and questioned his wife. She convinced them that she, not her husband, was the pastor—not an uncommon situation in China—and that the church had dispersed. She was the only one left, she told them. So to make an example of her, they took her to the police station and beat her until she was bloody and bruised.

As I listened to this pastor's story, I tried to imagine how I would react if that happened to my wife. That's a high price to pay for being in ministry, and quite honestly, I'm not sure how

I would respond. Frustration, anger, and a desire for vengeance would be hard to contain.

"How did you deal with it?" I asked.

I'll never forget his answer. "As we talked about it later, my wife said, 'Isn't it amazing that Jesus gave us the privilege to suffer for his sake and that we can make that kind of sacrifice to thank him for suffering for us?'"

I was glad I hadn't voiced my private thoughts of fear and vengeance while he was sharing his story. He was certainly looking at life through a different lens. He didn't see suffering necessarily as a negative; it was a way to express love for God and a normal aspect of following Jesus in that country. As I pondered our conversation on the long plane ride home, I realized how Americanized my view of sacrifice and suffering had become. We tend to avoid suffering at all costs. Yet those I admire most are often those who have sacrificed and suffered the most.

Something happens when we hear a story of great sacrifice. It's powerful and inspiring. It triggers a deep emotional response, even if we just read it in a book or see it in a movie. That's why the networks show those short features of Olympic athletes—the stories of a little girl who got up at three in the morning for years to practice for this very moment on the balance beam or the runner who overcame illness or extreme poverty to train for competition and a better life. I have to confess that I start tearing up when I hear those stories.

There's something about the Mother Teresas, Gandhis, and Martin Luther Kings of the world that stirs up higher, more noble dreams in us. It has always been that way; it's just how God made us. History is full of people who suffered under the persecution of others and, instead of becoming bitter or vengeful, forgave their enemies. When we see someone like Nelson Mandela spending twenty-five years in prison, finally being released, and showing no hint of retaliation, we stand in awe of the sacrifice that led to the end of apartheid. Every culture honors those who gave their life for a cause. In the church, we still look back to the early Christians who suffered at the hands of Roman emperors. The world is full of statues and stained glass windows commemorating the costly sacrifices people have made for something or someone greater than themselves.

Why do we feel such a magnetic pull toward people who make great sacrifices? What is this mystical connection between our soul and the nobility of selfless acts? I think the answer is that sacrifice is the clearest and greatest evidence of the extent of one's love and devotion toward a person, a cause, or a thing. Jesus said as much to his disciples: "Greater love has no one than this, that he lay down his life for his friends" (John 15:13). When someone pays the ultimate price for unselfish reasons, the depth of his or her love is clear. The measure of our sacrifice demonstrates what matters most.

The Measure of Love

I saw a great illustration of this principle on an Animal Planet television show recently. A small lioness was having trouble getting food for her cubs, but she finally killed her prey. Too small to drag the meal to her cubs, she went and got them to come to it. On the way back, seven or eight hyenas surrounded her and her babies. She had an opportunity to run, but she didn't. Faced with impossible odds, this lioness was willing to die in an attempt to save her cubs. And for reasons I can't explain, emotions swelled up inside of me as I saw her frantically swipe at hyenas attempting to attack her little ones. That kind of devotion is built into the design of creation. It resonates with us.

When we're truly devoted to someone or something, we're willing to make sacrifices. If you want to know what you really love, all you have to do is notice where you're giving your time, your energy, your money, and your dreams. For most people, that would involve some combination of spouse, children, job, and hobbies. If you're really good at something—playing an instrument, investing capital, painting pictures, building houses, playing a sport—you probably spent quite a bit of time and energy to be good at it. You may have natural talent in that area, and you may have enjoyed the process so much that it didn't seem like a sacrifice at all, but it still took the sacrifice of time, energy, and probably money. We gladly spend ourselves on what we love.

It's not hard to see how that principle applies to being a follower of Jesus. Whatever we have to offer, it will naturally flow in the direction of our deepest affections. The degree of our sacrifice corresponds to the degree of our love. Great Christians demonstrate great love by making great sacrifices.

Understanding Biblical Sacrifice and Worship

This concept is clear in the ministry of Jesus, but it was part of God's design from the very beginning. To understand it fully, we need to see how heavily it's emphasized throughout Scripture. Love and worship are intertwined in the sacrificial system of the Old Testament, and if we don't grasp the nature of the relationship between them, we miss both the significance of Jesus's sacrifice for us and the appropriate depth of our discipleship.

Leviticus is an instruction book for Israel's priests so they would know how to lead the nation in worship. It describes the required sacrifices to demonstrate love and respect for God. Five offerings are prescribed in the first ten chapters of Leviticus, and two were compulsory. One of the compulsory sacrifices was the sin offering—the sacrifice of a bull or a goat to atone for, or cover, your sin. The other was a guilt offering—another animal sacrifice to absolve your guilt. These were required at certain times, and everyone was expected to do them.

But the three voluntary offerings were an expression of faithfulness. The first was a burnt offering to express the depth of your devotion. The second was a grain offering given in gratitude for God's provision. When the crops were harvested, the first portion was brought to the altar and waved before the Lord in thanksgiving. The third was the peace offering, given simply to acknowledge how good God had been. The priest kept part of it, and the one making the offering ate the rest right there as a celebration of God's goodness.

What does that show us? First, access to God demands sacrifice; in order to come into his presence, you need to be atoned for—your sins covered. But after that, fellowship with God grows through sacrifice. Compulsory offerings made fellowship with God possible, but voluntary offerings were from the heart. They expressed the kind of love on which relationships are built.

Long before Leviticus, Abraham made an enormous sacrifice from the depths of his heart. God had promised him many descendants and then waited more than two decades to give him a son. Abraham tried waiting in faith. Then he attempted to help God out by fathering a son through his wife's maid—an effort that only made matters much worse. So Abraham went back to waiting in faith, though there must have been times when he wondered if God was ever going to follow through on his promise. But when Abraham was one hundred years old and his wife was ninety, Isaac was born and the promise seemed fulfilled.

Years later, however, God seemed to defy his own promise. He told Abraham to take Isaac to a mountaintop and sacrifice him. The miracle child, the "son of laughter" who represented the only means for God to fulfill his promise, was chosen as an offering by the same God. So Abraham did what great Christians do, even when they don't understand why or feel like they can; he obeyed. He got up early in the morning—it's best to obey early, because the motivation and courage may not be there later in the day—and set off with his son.

The journey from Abraham's home to the region of Moriah, the place God had designated for the sacrifice, probably wasn't very far geographically. But emotionally, it had to be the slowest, most arduous trip Abraham had ever taken. The beloved son who traveled at his side was, as far as Abraham knew, about to be killed by his father's own hand. Sacrifices don't get any greater than that.

"Where's the offering?" Isaac asked when they reached the mountain.

"The Lord will provide," Abraham answered with great faith. And he built an altar, tied Isaac to it, and raised his knife. He may initially have been incredibly confused by God's command, but he knew two things for certain: obedience was required, and God keeps his promises. One way or another, the contradiction would be reconciled—Hebrews 11:17–19 says Abraham believed he would receive Isaac back by resurrection. This was an incredibly difficult test.

The angel of the Lord appeared and told Abraham not to make the sacrifice. His priorities had been made clear. He was willing to sacrifice his only son, the beloved child he had anticipated for decades, because he loved God more (Gen. 22:1–18).

Why did God ask for Isaac? Abraham's son was the most precious thing he could have offered. His willingness to sacrifice him confirmed visibly what God already knew: Abraham worshiped God above all else. In effect, God asked Abraham who was more important, and Abraham pointed to God.

Don't think this was a unique question for only one man in history. God periodically tests every one of us for the singularity of our devotion through sacrifice. Every relationship you have, every possession you own, and every dream you aim to fulfill will have to go to the altar from time to time. It won't be a superficial test; it will hurt. Sacrifices always do. But it will demonstrate to you and others where your true love rests.

That sounds cruel to us, but God tests us out of his goodness and mercy. Most people wouldn't consider a command to sacrifice their precious child—or precious anything else, for that matter. But good people left unchecked with good things over time will drift away from God and embrace those good things as idols in their heart. And when that happens, their relationship with God—the source of true life—deteriorates. So when he taps us on the shoulder and says, "Give me that relationship, that job, that dream that you love," it's a merciful requirement. It keeps us close to him.

We resist this, of course, because we don't understand the difference between sacrifice and worship. In the chapter on taking great risks, I described how challenging it was for me to come to Walk Thru the Bible. Like most men, I spent the majority of my life trying to figure out what I was supposed to do. Then I went through that time that most men in their forties go through, questioning whether they're on the right track. I locked in on what I thought was the answer, and by God's grace he gave me a window of opportunity to do it with a great team of people at Santa Cruz Bible Church. We got all the right buildings we needed, the radio ministry popped up out of nowhere, I became great friends with several pastors, we developed a large staff, my kids got to surf, and for ten years I thought I was finally learning how to do what God had called me to do for a long time.

Then God called me to lay all that down and go in a different direction. That made no sense to me. I explained things to him very thoroughly:

"Lord, my wife likes it here, my kids are going to move back here, and we're going to sing 'Kumbaya' around the table every Thanksgiving. I've been obedient and I want your will to be here—my way. We've got it all planned."

His response was rather blunt. "If anyone comes to me and does not hate his father and mother, his wife and children, his brothers and sisters—yes, even his own life—he cannot be my disciple. And anyone who does not carry his cross and follow me cannot be my disciple" (Luke 14:26–27).

Some things in Scripture are hard to understand, but this isn't one of them. It's tough to do, but it's not complicated. Jesus made it clear that following him, even when that contradicts everything else that's important to us, is the top priority. When he told his disciples they had to be willing to carry a cross, he didn't mean they should just wear a chain around their neck. The cross was the equivalent of going to the electric chair or being given a lethal injection; it was a common way for criminals to die. Following Jesus means letting our agenda die and picking his up instead. And if following him isn't our ultimate, overriding purpose, we can't be a disciple. In other words, to love and worship Jesus is to put him above every relationship and issue in our life. It requires absolute sacrifice.

Jesus followed up his cross-carrying requirement with illustrations of what it means to count the cost. Tower builders need to estimate the cost before they lay the foundation. Otherwise, they'll be ridiculed for starting a project they can't finish.

A king has to calculate the strength of his army before going to war, and if his army is outnumbered or outarmed, he'll have to negotiate peace. Discipleship, Jesus said, is no different. There's a high cost involved in following him, and his disciples need to know that going into it. "Any of you who does not give up everything he has cannot be my disciple" (Luke 14:33). To love him is to sacrifice for him. Cheap worship is an oxymoron. It doesn't exist.

When God called me to move to Atlanta and lead Walk Thru the Bible, it was more than a career decision. My worship was at stake. I realized that the wife God had given me as a precious, wonderful gift had, over time, begun to take top position in my heart. I wanted to please her. God tested that relationship, and submitting it to him has, in retrospect, been the best possible thing for our marriage. I can't imagine our relationship being better than it is now. Obedience to God's direction brought us to the next level of maturity in our relationship with God and with each other.

When I teach on this, people get really nervous. I see them become restless in their seats. *Everything*, after all, is a really big word. It includes your most precious relationships, the career you've worked really hard to develop, the location you never want to move away from, and everything else you hold dear. But if we really understand who Jesus is, and if we really grasp the depth of his goodness and compassion, we realize that he only asks us to leave *everything* behind because, compared to him, *everything* is second rate.

Learn the Lesson of Plastic Pearls

Imagine seeing a little girl playing with a string of plastic beads. She loves it; it's one of her favorite toys. How would you feel if you asked her to give you her beads in exchange for an expensive necklace of real pearls, and she refused the gift? Logically, her attachment to her toy doesn't make sense. She would lose very little and gain so much more if she accepted your offer. One day, she would look back on the exchange, be grateful for the real pearls, and wonder why it was ever a tough decision. But she can't see all that. In her childish naiveté, all she knows is that she likes her plastic beads. Convincing her to give them up would be a very hard sell.

That's how many of us think, especially those of us who live in places where Christians are not persecuted. Pain helps a person discern between plastic and pearls, but we who live comfortably as Christians have trouble telling the difference. We hang onto our careers, families, and income as though they were the ultimate treasure. When God asks, "Do you love me more than these?" we can hardly believe a good God would confront us with that question. We're afraid to relinquish our toys for valuable pearls for two reasons: we're just not sure he really understands the value of our toys, and we're suspicious that the pearls aren't real. Meanwhile, God says, "I really love you, I want the best for you, and keeping me first in your heart is a treasure greater than you can imagine. It's worth any sacrifice you can conceive of."

Living Sacrifices

Paul was intimately familiar with this kind of sacrifice. He saw it as the appropriate response to God's mercy and an act of true worship. "I urge you," he wrote to Christians in Rome, "in view of God's mercy, to offer your bodies as living sacrifices, holy and pleasing to God—this is your spiritual act of worship" (Rom. 12:1).

Did you notice the motivation for this act of worship? It's "in view of God's mercy"—a grateful response that acknowledges the worthiness of God for all that he has done for us. When Paul says "to offer" our bodies as a living sacrifice, the word literally means "to present" yourself. It's the same word used in the Greek version of the Old Testament for the offering presented by the priest at the altar of sacrifice.

Paul's logical progression from the beginning of Romans has led up to this picture of sacrifice. Chapters 1–3 demonstrate that everyone has a problem with sin, but God solved that problem through the gift of Christ on the cross. Chapters 4–5 discuss how to receive that free gift by faith, and then 6–8 tell how by dying with him, we're raised with him to new life and now live in the power of his Spirit. Chapters 9–11 answer the question of Israel—how this salvation relates to God's special plan for the Hebrew people and how it ties in to his dealings with Israel in the past. And then chapter 12 begins the section of the letter that answers the question, "Now what?" In light of all that God has done, how does he want us to live?

The answer is in the very first verse of that chapter. "Present your bodies a living and holy sacrifice, acceptable to God, which is your spiritual service of worship" (Rom. 12:1 NASB). God wants us to offer ourselves. He doesn't just want our job, our money, or our stuff. He wants all of us—lock, stock, and barrel. The picture is of those voluntary offerings of devotion described in Leviticus, only in this case the offering is not a dead animal but a grateful servant who continues to live as God's own possession. It can't be given just on Sundays or any other time of the week. It's twenty-four hours a day, seven days a week, 365 days a year. The tense of the verb implies a moment of decision when you say, "Lord, all that I am is yours." It is an act of surrender to the lordship of Christ. Not unlike marriage, it's a particular point in time when you surrender yourself to another person, realizing that you must reaffirm and live out that commitment for the rest of your life.

We don't live in an agrarian society, so this picture of offering the first grain from the harvest or the best animal of the flock is a little foreign to us. I envision the modern-day equivalent to be like seeing your entire life as a blank check—then in view of your love for God and confidence in his goodness to you, signing the bottom of the check. Then you take the check, slide it under the door of heaven's throne room, and say, "Lord, fill it out however you want to. You tell me what you want me to do, where you want me to go, what you want me to give, and who you want me to serve. Whatever you write on the top of the check, that's what I'll do."

This is the normal Christian life. It's not the *typical* Christian life, by any means; many have completely neglected the teaching of this principle. But when Jesus said to follow him, this is what he intended. We call it *lordship* or *dedication*—a necessary part of the sanctification process that we experience after we're saved. It's the basis for living by faith.

I remember when I first heard someone explain Romans 12:1 and how Abraham's life illustrated the principle of a living sacrifice. It was 1975 at a conference at Penn State University. I had been born again over two years earlier, and I knew my sins were forgiven. I had been going to Bible study every Thursday night—and on Fridays and Saturdays I hit the bars with my teammates. Like a lot of Christians, I was living with one foot in the kingdom of God and one foot in the world. And I was miserable.

When I learned how worship and sacrifice work together, I realized that this was my missing ingredient. That's why the Christian life seemed so difficult. I was busy doing all the duties I knew I was supposed to be doing, like reading my Bible, praying, going to church, memorizing verses, and so on, not realizing that what God really wanted was me—every bit of me, all the time. So sitting on the floor with a group of people going through Romans 12, I told God that I was signing the bottom of the check. Whatever he wanted me to do, wherever he wanted me to go, I would obey.

That scared me to death, and I think most people can relate. Fear is the primary reason most of us have a very difficult time unreservedly offering ourselves as a living sacrifice. There's always something we want to hang onto—maybe it's a relationship, a career, or even a lifestyle—and we're afraid God will make us give it up. Lingering in the back of our minds is the thought that he might even send us to Africa, where we'd have to live with snakes and eat food we don't recognize. And while guidance like that is certainly possible, God probably has something in mind that will fit us and fulfill us better than what we've planned for ourselves. He's not interested in making us all do something we hate. He just wants us to be willing to do whatever he says, even when it costs us a lot.

Intellectually, we know that. His will, even when it's hard, is never bad for us. But emotionally, we wrestle with the thought that surrendering our will to his is going to cause us more pain than joy. It's the same dynamic we experienced as kids when our parents made us eat our vegetables. We knew they were right; a good diet really was best for us. But we were convinced we wouldn't enjoy it, and the benefits would be too far in the future to motivate us immediately. When this dynamic plays out in our relationship with God, the issues are much larger. We can spend a big part of our lives wrestling with the fear of forfeiting all our desires when we sign the bottom of the blank check and offer it to God.

If you're struggling with that decision in some area of your life right now, let me encourage you. It's true that the sacrifices involved are very real, but it's also true that the benefits are worth the costs. Jesus promised great rewards, both in this age and the age to come, for those who surrender everything to him (Mark 10:29–30). God never uses a blank check selfishly. He always takes care of the one who signed it.

Since that day of commitment in 1975, I've sought to be completely God's. As with everyone who makes that decision, it hasn't always been easy. It seems like every time I take three steps forward, I take at least two backward. I've followed Jesus very imperfectly. But the bottom line is that when he taps me on the shoulder, like he did about the opportunity at Walk Thru the Bible, whether I'm going to obey is not the question. I may have to work through my willingness—I may even ask him twenty times if I heard him correctly—but the check was signed a long time ago. He has every right to fill in the blank however he wants to.

Have you ever made that decision? Has there been a certain time on a certain day when you've specifically said something like this to God? "Lord, I'm yours, a living and holy sacrifice. Here's the check. I submit myself to your will, and you have complete freedom to do whatever you want to do in my life without my resistance."

The stronger your personality, the harder this is to do. For those of us who border on being control freaks, coming to that decision can be a real tug-of-war. It certainly was for me. But I can assure you that it's the smartest, most emotionally satisfying decision you'll ever make for at least two reasons. First, you won't be disappointed by trusting God's wisdom for your life because he wants the very best for you and knows what it is. Second, the alternative is an unconscious decision to be the CEO of your own life and call all the shots—which, of course, would be completely irrational. If you find it difficult to offer yourself as a living sacrifice, consider the alternative. People who refuse to submit to God and choose to run their own lives ultimately end up unfulfilled. Yes, presenting yourself as a living sacrifice will cost you everything. But *not* offering yourself will cost you even more.

What Motivates Great Christians?

Jesus said that the greatest love is to lay down one's life for another. That's what he did for us, and he calls us to do the same for him. When he defined following him as dying to self and taking up a cross daily, he was speaking to a large crowd. This is a command for every follower of Christ; becoming a living sacrifice is the normal Christian life. But how do we get there? What is it that motivates great Christians to make great sacrifices?

The first few decades of church history turned the world upside down. The followers of Jesus who became living sacrifices changed the entire culture around them because they were willing to be ravaged by lions in an arena, to minister to diseased, dying people at the risk of their own lives, and to relinquish anything they had for the sake of the kingdom. They made great sacrifices, not only because it was the right thing to do, but because they *wanted* to. Like the apostles in Acts 5:41, they rejoiced that they were worthy to suffer for Christ. They had such love for him that sacrifice flowed naturally from their lives.

That, I believe, is one of the key differences between good and great Christians. All Christians, of course, are called to offer their entire lives to Jesus, and no Christian does that perfectly. But some seem to follow Jesus with joyful, reckless abandon.

Those are the ones whose offering as a living sacrifice is more consistent and longer lasting. It's one thing to sacrifice everything for Jesus and another to sacrifice everything zealously. The latter kind of offering seems to be able to endure more hardship and carry more power.

All Christians need to realize that we're living in a little slice of eternity called "time." You can live an average life—or even a much-better-than-average life—and leave a legacy in your window of time that lasts a few decades, a few generations, or maybe even a few centuries. But unless you're a living sacrifice on the altar of God, you won't leave an eternal legacy. The only way to bear fruit that lasts forever is to have the kind of love for God that lays everything down for him. That kind of radical disciple is the kind who revolutionizes the world.

Good Christians make the sacrifice required to demonstrate that Jesus is, in fact, the object of their worship. But great Christians go above and beyond everything that's required to express their overflowing love and commitment to Christ. Beyond their fear and anxiety about surrendering every dream and desire to him, they trust God to take what he already owns—their life—and do something lasting and wonderfully fulfilling with it. Great Christians do what's required, and then they voluntarily go over and above what is required to express the depth of their love for their heavenly Father and their relationship with Christ.

I have an amazing relationship with my bank. I put money in my account, and then later when I go up to the counter and ask to withdraw a thousand dollars, the teller just gives it to me. I don't need to explain what I'm going to use it for or justify my desire for it. She doesn't say, "What? Who do you think you are, demanding a thousand bucks like that? Manager! This guy is trying to take a lot of money from our bank!" And if any teller ever did say that, the manager would walk up and explain: "It's his money, so he can take it out any time he wants."

God tries to have that kind of relationship with us, but we often resist him. We'll give everything if we have to, just as that hypothetical teller reluctantly hands over all the money I've asked for. But most real tellers give me my withdrawal cheerfully and willingly. As Paul asked, "What do you have that you did not receive?" (1 Cor. 4:7). The answer, of course, is "nothing." Everything is a gift from the Lord. So if life, breath, money, jobs, skills, gifts, relationships, and everything else are given by God, why do we get so upset when he wants to make a withdrawal? Like the early Christians, we wouldn't if we understood God's love, the nature of his relationship with us, the benefits he promises, and his sovereign ownership of all that exists.

Unconditional Love

I've found four truths that underlie the motivation of great Christians to eagerly offer themselves as living sacrifices, and the first is an understanding of God's unconditional love. Great Christians are not caught in the performance trap, trying to earn brownie points with God. They understand that they are totally, unconditionally loved apart from their works. Their sacrifice is a response to that love. It comes not from a sense of duty but from a sense of gratitude for the relationship. When people have a deep sense of brokenness over their own sin and understand their indebtedness to God's grace and mercy, overflowing love is a natural response.

David was a great lover of God. He acknowledged his sinfulness with Bathsheba and was deeply grieved before God for what he had done. In complete brokenness, he cried out to God in a psalm of repentance. He came to God with an attitude that said, "I've blown it and I don't deserve anything," and he knew how God would respond: "A broken and contrite heart, O God, you will not despise" (Ps. 51:17).

We see the same principle with Paul. What motivated him to preach the gospel and start churches all over southern Europe and the Near East—even under frequent persecution, floggings to the point of death, shipwreck, and imprisonment on many occasions? "I was shown mercy so that in me, the worst of sinners, Christ Jesus might display his unlimited patience as an example for those who would believe on him and receive eternal life" (1 Tim. 1:16). Paul knew he was a debtor to grace. There seemed to be no evidence in his life of reluctance to serve

Christ. There was no "have to, ought to, supposed to, need to."
His service was all out of relationship.

There's a great story in Luke 7 that illustrates this response
to God's unconditional love. Jesus was at a dinner hosted by
Simon the Pharisee when a woman with a very bad reputation
came into the house—uninvited, of course—and began weeping
on Jesus's feet and wiping them with her hair. Then she broke a
very expensive jar of perfume—possibly worth an entire year's
wages—and poured it out on his feet. That was a sure sign to
Simon that Jesus was not a prophet. This woman was obviously
a sinner, and a good Jewish teacher would never let such an
impure person touch him. Jesus knew what Simon was thinking and told him, "Her many sins have been forgiven—for she
loved much. But he who has been forgiven little loves little"
(Luke 7:47).

The point of Jesus's teaching is not that some people are
more forgiven than others; we're all forgiven completely when
we come to Christ. But this woman recognized the depth of her
sin, and that caused her to recognize the depth of Jesus's love.
When someone has deep devotion and tenderness toward God,
that person almost always has tremendous pain in their past
and a dramatic experience of God's forgiveness. They trust in
God's love not just with their head but also with their heart.

God's Relational Economy

Not only do great Christians grasp God's unconditional love,
but the second truth that underlies the motivation of great
Christians to offer themselves as living sacrifices is that they
also embrace his relational economy. When God measures our
love and devotion, he doesn't look at the size of our gifts. He
looks at the size of our sacrifice.

The classic example of this in Scripture is the story in Luke
21:1–4 of the widow who put two small coins into the temple
treasury. The rich were offering large amounts to fund temple
activities, and this woman deposited two pieces of the nation's
smallest currency. But her gift, Jesus said, was more than all the
others because it was all she had to live on. Widows in that day

had no way to support themselves, and she could have easily justified giving nothing. No one would have blamed her. But out of love, she gave all she had, and Jesus got excited about it. He pointed her out to his disciples and made her an object lesson in the eternal Word of God.

If you were making $20,000 and trying to support three children, your financial situation would be rather tight. A tithe of $2,000 would be a significant sacrifice. But if you made $100,000, a tithe wouldn't be quite so sacrificial, would it? Double that salary, and although a tithe of $20,000 sounds like a huge donation, no one should have a problem squeaking by on the other $180,000. In this case, $20,000 is a great amount to give, but it's not a huge sacrifice.

I remember talking to a man who was really excited and proud about giving ten million dollars to the work of the Lord. Knowing that was about a tenth of his net worth, I asked how much his life changed by sacrificing ten million. The answer, of course, was "not at all." I'm certainly not criticizing such a generous gift. Giving ten million dollars is wonderful. Praise God for that kind of faithfulness. I'm just suggesting that this was an offering, not a sacrifice. We can't confuse 10 percent of an enormous income with devotion and sacrifice.

Great Christians aren't content with dutifully giving 10 percent of their income. When God increases their resources, they ask him for more opportunities to give. Not only does the amount of their giving increase, so does the proportion. They don't do it because they have to or in order to earn points with God. It's an opportunity to express their love. They want to give extravagantly because they love him.

Eternal Goodness

The third truth that motivates great Christians to make great sacrifices is that they are convinced of God's eternal goodness. They hold an absolute, unwavering conviction that the rewards for laying down their life for God far outweigh the cost.

In Mark 10:28–31 Jesus has just let a young man walk away from him because the man could not bring himself to let go of the idol of his heart: his possessions. Peter, not known for his subtleties, reminds Jesus that he and the other disciples have left everything for him. His remark, in other words, asks, "What's in it for us?"

Jesus assured him,

> No one who has left home or brothers or sisters or mother or father or children or fields for me and the gospel will fail to receive a hundred times as much in this present age (homes, brothers, sisters, mothers, children and fields—and with them, persecutions) and in the age to come, eternal life.
>
> Mark 10:29–30

Notice that Jesus says "for me." This is sacrifice at a relational level. Some people may make great sacrifices for a cause or to enlarge their spiritual ego, but Jesus is talking about the kind of sacrifice that flows out of love for him. And when that's the case, the rewards far exceed the costs.

Paul understood this. "I consider that our present sufferings are not worth comparing with the glory that will be revealed in us," he wrote (Rom. 8:18). Many of us today act as if heaven and spiritual rewards are afterthoughts. We may say we believe that this life isn't all there is, but we keep desperately pursuing its treasures as though it is. We keep holding onto our plastic beads as though we aren't sure that the real pearls are out there. We look for the minimum requirements of sacrifice simply because we want to be right with God. But God isn't looking for minimum Christians. He wants people who will take off the beads because they love him and they know the pearls he offers will be better.

I'm in awe of the sacrifices made by many of the great Christians around the world associated with Walk Thru the Bible. One of our teachers in a country hostile to Christianity brings fifteen people at a time into a soundproof room to teach discipleship courses because if he gets caught, he will be killed. One of our leaders in Southeast Asia is a former insurance magnate who walked away from a multimillion-dollar enterprise. He closed down his business and decided that he'd use his gift of networking for the Lord instead of for income. We pay him only a dollar a year for his leadership. Why? Because he loves serving the Lord, and he believes God is good.

I have a good friend who is quite wealthy, and he kept using a phrase I didn't understand at first: "How many steaks can you eat in one day?" What he meant was that there's only so much pleasure one person can enjoy. After a certain saturation point, continued spending on oneself has no benefit. My friend would much rather spend his money and his life in a way that really matters.

Great Christians understand that the goal is to die with a zero balance. There's nothing wrong with leaving an honorable and reasonable inheritance for your children, but everything else will do you no good. Why not leverage it for eternal purposes? Toward the end of his life, Campus Crusade for Christ founder Bill Bright emptied his retirement account to fund ministry in Ukraine. Most of us would worry about how to support ourselves in our later years, but he figured God would provide one way or another. That was great because it wasn't required. It was over and above, because those are the kinds of sacrifices great Christians make.

It's All His

The fourth conviction of those who make great sacrifices is that they recognize God's sovereign ownership. They don't consider sacrifice praiseworthy, as though the offering is a noble act. They consider it a privilege because it all belongs to God anyway.

In Luke 17:7–10 Jesus told a parable about how a master reacts when a servant comes in from the field. The master doesn't give the servant the royal treatment for doing what he was hired to do in the first place, and the servant doesn't expect him to. Our obedience is like that, Jesus said. People who make great sacrifices don't think they deserve special treatment or a great reward. They realize that they're just regular people.

When the people of Israel brought offerings to King David for the future building of the temple, they gave freely and wholeheartedly to the Lord. David rejoiced, and in his praises to God, he said, "Who am I, and who are my people, that we should be able to give as generously as this? Everything comes from you, and we have given you only what comes from your hand" (1 Chron. 29:14). David believed in God's sovereign ownership of all things. The tribes of Israel had only given God material he had created and blessed them with. It all came from him, so it only made sense that it be given back to him extravagantly.

The world doesn't understand this kind of sacrifice. It seems like such a waste to give up things like success, health, possessions, and comfort. But that's the kind of offering God blesses with extraordinary power. David Brainerd, for example, was an early missionary to the Native Americans of the Northeast. He lived among them in a forest while his health deteriorated in cold New England winters. He died at twenty-nine, having seen only a handful of converts. But God used Brainerd's diary to prompt William Carey, Henry Martyn, and scores of other young men and women to go to the far reaches of the world with the message of the gospel.

William Borden is another example. This promising Yale graduate sensed God's call to leave his prospects for worldly success at the age of twenty-five and go to Egypt as a missionary. He died of cerebral meningitis within weeks of his arrival, and few people could see beyond the futility of his act of devotion. But God used his story to move thousands to action. They saw eternal values in the dreams of a young man who loved Jesus, and it inspired their love as well.

The Measure of Your Love

Take the temperature of your heart right now. Are you growing in your love for Jesus? Do you understand how unconditionally he loves you? Do you operate in his relational economy? If you signed the bottom of a blank check to him, could you trust him to be relentlessly good to you in return? Have you considered that everything in your life comes from him anyway? How tightly are you clinging to your plastic beads?

God's kingdom is about extravagant love. He made the ultimate sacrifice for us by sending Jesus to die an excruciating death on a cross as payment for our sins. He looks for those who will love him extravagantly in return. A sacrifice is merely love with clothes on. Abraham demonstrated great love when he offered his son, Isaac, and Paul urged us to lay our lives on the altar and called it an act of worship. Why? Because love and sacrifice go hand in hand.

How great is your love? You can easily answer that question by looking at how much you sacrifice for the Lord. If you want to be a good Christian, sacrifice everything. If you want to be a great Christian, sacrifice everything with a passion.

Action Steps

1. Think of someone you know who has made a great sacrifice, either for the Lord or for someone else. Designate a time to talk with that person and ask him or her how that sacrifice felt (1) right before it was made, (2) right after it was made, and (3) now, looking back on it. If you are facing a similar decision of commitment or sacrifice and are comfortable doing so, ask the person for counsel and prayer.
2. Ask God this week to highlight for you one area of your life that is not fully surrendered to him. When that area becomes clear to you, pray a prayer of surrender, offering yourself completely to the Lord. Then think of one outward act that would demonstrate surrender in that area and do it.
3. Memorize Luke 14:33, "Any of you who does not give up everything he has cannot be my disciple."

Questions for Reflection and Discussion

1. In what area of your life have you wrestled most intensely with a fear of surrendering everything to God? What scares you about signing a blank check for him to fill out?
2. Think about the acts of obedience you've done in the last week—Bible study, serving in the church, worship services, and so on. What motives were behind each of them? What was your level of enthusiasm for each one? Did they flow out of a sense of obligation, love, or a combination of the two?
3. What attitudes toward hardship did New Testament Christians seem to have? (Read Acts 5:40–41 for one remarkable example.) Why do you think they were so recklessly abandoned to God's purposes? In what ways can you become more like them?

8

Enjoy Great Moments

I got a note in the mail last year from a man I hadn't heard from in twenty-five years. He was my basketball coach in college, and at the time he was not a believer. He was walking through a Christian bookstore recently and saw a book with my name on it. He picked it up and read a section that had some stories from college, realized that this was in fact that skinny guy he remembered, and decided to write me a note.

"I read your book and went to your website," he wrote. "I see your life is moving very fast. I want you to know that I've come to Christ and I'm really proud of you. Just remember: everything starts with balance." I could almost hear his voice. Defense starts with balance, good shots start with balance, . . . and most importantly, life has to have balance. The lesson was deeply ingrained in my mind.

In the last few chapters, we've talked about some things that really push us spiritually. Great sacrifices, great risks, great prayers—these are heavy issues. If heaviness is always the tone of your life, you'll be out of balance, and a lot of other areas of your life will be negatively affected. That's not the path to greatness. This may be hard to believe, but moving from good to great requires the ability to enjoy great moments.

"Joy is the serious business of heaven," C. S. Lewis once wrote.[1] A lot of people don't believe that. In fact, this quote makes some people really uncomfortable, as though the idea of enjoying life might be almost illegal—or at least frowned upon in the kingdom of God. After all, the Christian life deals with life-and-death issues that have eternal implications. Sin is serious; Jesus's death on the cross is serious; the Great Commission is serious—which is why the Bible tells us to be spiritually sober and alert so often, right? (See in the NASB 1 Cor. 15:34; 16:13; Eph. 6:18; Col. 4:2; 1 Thess. 5:6, 8; 2 Tim. 4:5; 1 Peter 1:13; 4:7; 5:8.)

That's true, but truth out of balance is not the whole truth. My coach sent me the same message he taught in college because he knew it had implications beyond the world of sports. Maybe he remembered how intense I get when I'm focused on a goal, or maybe he was struggling with that issue himself. But he's right. Balance is important, even in our discipleship. Actually, *especially* in our discipleship.

Here's a question many Christians will never ask you: Are you enjoying your life? Are you deeply satisfied, drinking in rich experiences with people, places, and circumstances God is providentially surrounding you with? If you are, you're unusual. Most people are waiting to enjoy life after they finish their to-do list, after they marry the right person or get the right job, after they raise their kids the right way, or after they retire. We're always waiting for the next big thing—the next purchase or position or place. But enjoyment never comes; it's always right around the corner, but we never actually get there.

Great Christians do enjoy life. Believe it or not, the Bible teaches balance. If we think we can be great Christians with a life devoid of laughter, relaxation, and just plain fun, we've ignored huge portions of Scripture. Yes, we go through difficult seasons and endure painful hardships, and we have serious responsibilities to fulfill. But the backdrop for all of those temporary trials is a deep, lasting joy. Without it, we can't say we're being conformed to the image of Christ. We can't even say we're being biblical.

Here's what Solomon, the man Scripture calls the wisest person in the world, wrote:

> There is a time for everything,
>   and a season for every activity under heaven: . . .
> a time to weep and a time to laugh,
>   a time to mourn and a time to dance.
>
> Ecclesiastes 3:1, 4

He expands on that thought a few verses later:

> He has made everything beautiful in its time. He has also set eternity in the hearts of men; yet they cannot fathom what God has done from beginning to end. I know that there is nothing better for men than to be happy and do good while they live. That everyone may eat and drink, and find satisfaction in all his toil—this is the gift of God.
>
> Ecclesiastes 3:11–13

Did you catch that? Being happy and finding satisfaction are gifts from God. A lot of good Christians are busy and stressed and enduring hardship without understanding the joy that comes from God, but there aren't any *great Christians* like that. The New Testament is so full of reasons and reminders to rejoice that the absence of joy in a believer's life has to be considered negligent or even disobedient.

Do we need to be serious about following Jesus? Of course. Does that involve great sacrifices and constant discipline? Absolutely. But in the midst of a fallen world filled with pain and disappointment, we can rest in the absolute certainty that Jesus is coming back. We can drink deeply from his grace and his extravagant promises. And we can enjoy the gifts of God both now and forever.

Solomon went on to write about enjoying God's gifts in Ecclesiastes 5: "When God gives any man wealth and possessions, and enables him to enjoy them, to accept his lot and be happy in his work—this is a gift of God. He seldom reflects on the days of his life, because God keeps him occupied with gladness of heart" (vv. 19–20 NASB). Does that describe you? Are you occupied with gladness of heart? Are you filled with contentment from simply being alive, knowing God loves you, and seeing the opportunities he's placed before you? Or do you find yourself looking back with regret and looking forward with anxiety—busy and stressed, focused and driven, chasing after the happiness that never comes?

Notice that these questions aren't about being productive, making an impact, or being "spiritual." Those pursuits are certainly important, but they aren't evidence of contentment and joy. They can easily turn into "chasing after the wind," as Solomon describes it (Eccles. 1:17). The real issue is whether you are deeply enjoying the life God has given you. If I asked your spouse, your best friend, or one of your children if you were a happy person—someone who really enjoys life—how would they answer?

Great Christians are focused and disciplined, making great sacrifices and taking great risks. They get a lot done, but they're also fun to be around. They know how to kick back and have a great time. Sometimes they'll just stop, take a break from the rat race, and thank God for the richness of his gifts. Then they'll get back on track and do what he wants them to do. They understand that joy is the serious business of heaven.

Your Joy Matters to God

Some people act as if they need permission to start enjoying life. If that's how you feel, let me share with you biblically why God not only allows you to enjoy great moments, he encourages you to. This is not a *should*, it's a *must*. It's God's desire for his people.

I believe Scripture gives us at least five reasons that we are to enjoy great moments both for our own well-being and to fulfill God's purposes. My hope is that by the end of this chapter, you'll realize how vital—and biblical—it is to enjoy life now!

1. *It reminds us of God's goodness*. Psalm 84:11 (NASB) says,

> For the LORD God is a sun and shield;
> The LORD gives grace and glory;
> No good thing does He withhold from those who walk
> uprightly.

God is into giving good things to his people. The promise of this verse is that he has plenty to give and a desire to give it. But if we can't stop long enough to enjoy his gifts, we forget them. We take them for granted, turn our focus to all the challenges of life, and then struggle with all the anxieties that come from such a negative focus. When we enjoy God's blessings, it reminds us that all good things come from him. More than that, it reminds us that *he* is good.

2. *It sustains us in adversity*. The Book of Nehemiah describes the project to build Jerusalem's walls when Israel returned from captivity in Babylon. The first portion of the book chronicles the rebuilding of the physical structure, and the second half focuses on rebuilding the people. When the wall had been built, Ezra the priest read the books of Moses—the first five books of the Bible—to the assembly. Realizing how badly they had missed God's will and violated his commandments, they began to weep. Because the day was at the time of a prescribed festival, Nehemiah encouraged them with these words: "Go and enjoy choice food and sweet drinks, and send some to those who have nothing prepared. This day is sacred to our Lord. Do not grieve, for the joy of the LORD is your strength" (Neh. 8:10). So, according to the Word of God, they threw a party.

Nehemiah didn't dismiss the need to repent, but he understood that God had given the people a time of gladness. Sorrow was natural and necessary sometimes, but it couldn't define the life of God's people. God had given them reason to celebrate. The joy of the Lord was their strength. It's also ours.

3. *It honors God as the source of joy*. Enjoying great moments is important because it honors God, who is the source of all our joy. James 1:17 says, "Every good thing given and every perfect

gift is from above, coming down from the Father of lights, with whom there is no variation or shifting shadow" (NASB).

Let me share a hypothetical word picture with you—in other words, don't go looking for a chapter and verse. I envision getting to heaven one day and finding a big door with my name on it. When I open the door, I see shelves stacked high with beautifully wrapped gifts. "What's this?" I ask, and the Lord tells me it's all the good things he planned for me. "So this is what heaven has in store for us," I whisper in amazement. And the Lord says, "No, you don't understand. Heaven's much better than this. These are all the things I wanted you to have on earth, but I couldn't get you to look up and receive them. You were so busy trying to prove yourself to people, trying to make an impact, positioning yourself for the next career move, and all those intense stresses. I just wanted to refresh you and bless you and show you my love. You know those people who kept inviting you to dinner? They were some of my choicest servants. You'd have loved them. But your calendar was so full with producing that you never took time for enjoying, relating, and just relaxing. I put opportunities in your path that you never noticed, and I put people in your path who would have loved you if you'd given them the time. You just never took the time to slow down and receive what I was offering."

Does that sound farfetched? The logistics may be—I'm not sure exactly how heaven works—but the concept isn't. Enjoying great moments reminds us that God is the source of all of our joy, and that honors him.

4. *It connects our hearts to those we love*. We may enjoy some great moments when we're alone, but most of them are a shared experience. In Luke's account of the birth of Jesus, Mary enjoyed several great moments because of the people who recognized who her son was. After the shepherds reported what the angels had told them, she "treasured up all these things and pondered them in her heart" (Luke 2:19). Then when she and Joseph took Jesus to the temple to consecrate him to the Lord and offer a sacrifice, they encountered two people to whom the Holy Spirit had revealed Jesus's identity: a devout old man named Simeon, who had been waiting for years to see the Messiah,

and a woman named Anna, who had been fasting and praying and who thanked God for the child and told all the bystanders about him. And "the child's father and mother marveled at what was said about him" (Luke 2:33). Mary's heart connected with those to whom God had revealed the truth about her son, the Messiah. She treasured those experiences and marveled at them because other people were brought into the great moment in history God had given her.

We have little slices of time that fill us with joy—the birth of a baby, a beautiful sunset, a wedding day, graduation, the day we accepted Christ—and God wants us to treasure them. But we treasure them even more when we celebrate them with others, especially those close to our heart. They mean more when others are involved. I believe some of those early experiences sustained Mary for many years. As she watched Jesus die in agony, she may have pondered Simeon's words predicting the sword that would pierce her soul but also promising that her son would cause the falling and rising of many in Israel. When God puts people around us who affirm the gifts he has given, we connect with them—and him—in a deeper way.

Jesus demonstrated this too. On his last night before the cross, he told his disciples that he eagerly desired to eat the Passover meal with them (Luke 22:15). Being fully God, he knew what was ahead, and being fully human, he craved the fellowship of his friends. They ate together, sang together, cried together, and prayed together. He had a great moment with the people closest to him, and, to a degree, their shared experience helped sustain him during that long night. In the midst of impending torture, he connected with his friends.

5. *God uses the joy of great moments to renew us.* God even scheduled great moments through his law. As a child, I used to think of the Sabbath as a day when religious people couldn't do anything fun. Then I read the Bible and discovered that the Sabbath wasn't about what we can't do. It's God's way of telling us not to stress like unbelievers who feel they have to work seven days a week. He urges us to stop, rest, worship, kick back, take a deep breath, and enjoy one another. The Sabbath is a required vacation day because God knew we'd never get around to it as

an option. It's a chance to look back over the last week and say, "Isn't God good? Let's enjoy what he has given us."

That's how God renews our bodies with the joy of rest, but he also renews our hearts with laughter. I've known some Christians who were so serious that no one could really enjoy being around them. In fact, I used to be one of them myself. Early in my Christian life, I became so serious and intense about Bible study, Scripture memory, and keeping all the rules that a non-Christian friend told me, "If your life is what a committed Christian looks like, I don't want to have anything to do with Christianity." We forget that Jesus seemed to be the easiest person on the planet to hang out with. Some of his plays on words were really humorous, and I'm quite sure Peter, John, and the other disciples had a good laugh with him over some of those. If we're made in the image of God and we enjoy laughing and having fun, doesn't it stand to reason that God enjoys that too?

In spite of the fact that many people draw a thick line between laughter and spirituality, the Bible doesn't. "A cheerful heart is good medicine, but a crushed spirit dries up the bones" (Prov. 17:22). That's one of those verses that modern science confirms completely. Laughter builds the immune system and restores health. God designed us to enjoy life.

You may find a lot of anguish and confusion in the Psalms, but you'll find more praise and gratitude. Some psalms are completely dedicated to praise, worship, and giving thanks, and there's plenty of encouragement in them to play trumpets loudly, get out the tambourines and the stringed instruments, and dance, dance, dance. If you wanted to eliminate fun and celebration from the Bible, you'd have to cut a lot of passages out of it. Life is an enjoyable gift.

So Why Don't We?

If enjoying life is a gift, an expectation, and an integral part of how we were made, why are so many of us discouraged all the time and weighed down with seriousness? How have normal, committed Christians like us been trained to miss out on so much of the good things and good times God wants us to enjoy? As I look back on my own struggles in this area, I think at least three factors undermine our ability to enjoy great moments: a distorted view of God, a warped theology of pleasure, and an unwillingness to face our false beliefs and unhealthy behavior patterns.

A Distorted View of God

Mirrors in the funhouse at a carnival can make you look ten times fatter than you are or ten times skinnier—or both at the same time for different parts of your body. It's a lot of fun to see your friends and yourself with gross distortions, but it can really mess up our lives when we see God that way. Even when we know what the Bible says about him, we have a tendency to magnify some attributes and minimize others. The result is a view of God that has the right characteristics in the wrong proportions.

The parable of the prodigal son in Luke 15 can help return balance to our perspective of God. It's the story of a young man who demanded his inheritance, rejected his father, and went away to spend all his money in reckless, sinful living. Soon destitute, he came to his senses and decided that returning home in humiliation was better than remaining independent in poverty. So he practiced his repentant speech and went home with his hat in his hands, hoping to at least be hired as a servant.

While he was still a long way off, his father abandoned all dignity and cultural norms to run and throw his arms around his boy. He gave him a robe, a ring, and sandals, insisted that he return as a son and not a servant, and threw a big party in his honor. The father lavished his love and forgiveness on the son who had once offended him. And that's usually where we end the story.

But Scripture doesn't end the story there. The older brother hears the music and dancing from the party and asks one of the servants what's happening. When he finds out that his rude, rebellious little brother is getting the royal treatment from Dad, he's furious. He can't believe that after all of his good behavior and hard work, the black sheep of the family gets to have a party. His father has to explain to him that his brother was dead and is now alive, that he suffered severe consequences for his corrupt lifestyle and is now reaping the benefits of extravagant mercy. And in his explanation, the father makes a statement that we rarely give much attention to: "You are always with me, and everything I have is yours" (Luke 15:31).

The older son had a distorted view of his father, and this is how his father corrected him. He could have thrown a party any time he wanted to. He could have asked his father if it was okay to invite some friends over, kill a fatted calf, and have a ball. Apparently he didn't ever do that; he was too busy earning the father's favor to realize he already had it. He was so absorbed with his performance that he could never enjoy life.

We do that with God, forgetting that our life is about enjoying a relationship we already have, not establishing one we hope to have. We spend all our energy and time trying to prove ourselves to God or even to parents, bosses, or someone in our past who made us feel like we'll never amount to anything. Instead of having a godly drive to move forward and bear fruit, we become driven to accomplish and achieve. Some of the most committed Christians I know are zealous and diligent to get everything right in their own lives and meet all the needs of everyone they know, but there's no joy in their life. That's a problem. Being driven to perform may get a lot accomplished, but there's a subtle, self-righteous arrogance in it. It comes from a warped distortion of the Father's heart.

I wish I learned this lesson from reading a great book, but I learned it instead from some hard experiences. I spent years as an elder-brother Christian because I believed some lies about God. One of the biggest was that being godly meant always giving up my desires and plans to do what others want, because a servant always puts others first. Sounds true, doesn't it? But the truth is that I must be *willing* to give up my plans in submission to God's direction in serving and loving others. But the plans and dreams I have are important as well; many of them are God-given. And part of loving others is allowing them to love me—even giving them an opportunity to make sacrifices for me, as I make sacrifices for them, if God so leads.

When you believe the lie that you always need to submit your will to everyone else's, the result is a never-ending to-do list. You never give yourself time to enjoy the gifts God has surrounded you with. When you don't experience joy, you don't have the strength of the Lord, and you end up in a performance trap that's steeped in self-effort and absolutely no fun.

One of the sad consequences of this kind of life is the temptation it often leads to. When you hear a story of a faithful, consistent Christian—often even a leader in the church—who suddenly is separated from his wife, driving a red sports car, and running around with someone half his age, I can almost guarantee that he has lived with an elder-brother mentality for years and was never able to enjoy life. The suppression of genuine, God-ordained pleasure is frustrating and depressing, and those who live with it long enough eventually explode—sometimes in very ungodly ways.

That's what a distorted view of God can lead to. The truth is that God's gifts are always available to his children, and he welcomes—even implores—our enjoyment of them.

A Warped Theology of Pleasure

Pleasure has been polluted and distorted to the degree that many consider it the opposite of godliness. That's one of the subtle ways Satan has corrupted the goodness of God's creation; it's godliness versus pleasure, and people think they have to make a choice.

What's the truth that replaces that lie? The Bible teaches that it is ungodly to pursue sensual desires like food, sex, materialism, fame, money, and status in order to feed your soul or make you feel like somebody important. That's called hedonism, and it usually takes no consideration for whether sensual desires fit within God's design for them. It's a live-for-today, go-for-the-gusto philosophy, and it exalts worldly pleasure above godliness. But Scripture teaches that there's more fulfilling, lasting pleasure in living life according to God's design. In fact, God invented pleasure. He has the only keys to the real thing.

Jonathan Edwards was a great Christian who knew the importance of enjoying great moments. That may be hard to imagine for many people who wrongly see this Puritan as a stern and sour taskmaster of the faith—the Christian version of the Pharisees of Jesus's day. But consider what Edwards said about God-given pleasures: "It is not contrary to Christianity that a man should love himself, or, which is the same thing, should love his own happiness. . . . The saints love their own happiness. Yea, those that are perfect in happiness, the saints and angels in heaven, love their own happiness; otherwise that happiness which God hath given them would be no happiness to them."[2] If a sober-minded eighteenth-century Puritan could take time to delight in the God-given pleasures of life, as Edwards did, surely we can too.

C. S. Lewis said that the problem with Christians is not that we enjoy too much pleasure but that we enjoy too little.[3] We've equated pleasure with sin, and that makes it hard to have fun or relax without feeling guilty about it. We even refer to many of our enjoyments as "guilty pleasures." We've reacted to that false association by throwing the baby out with the bathwater. Few Christians know how to stop and soak in all the good things God has given. Lewis was right. In thinking of pleasure as sinful, we've stayed too far away from it. We experience too little of the pleasures God designed us to enjoy.

Pleasure is a harsh taskmaster but an excellent tour guide. That one line sums it up for me and helps me keep a balanced perspective. If you think you'll be happy once you get the big house, the boat, the remodeled kitchen, the second house, the right position at work, the exotic vacation, the plastic surgery, a better sex life—fill in the blank with whatever is appropriate to your situation—pleasure will become a harsh taskmaster. It's like a drug. No matter what kind of hit you get, you'll need a bigger one to satisfy you next time.

But pleasure is an excellent tour guide along the road of life. When you walk with God and are able to stop and enjoy what he has provided, you get refreshed and renewed. In the midst of a fallen world full of difficulty and pain, you need to be able to kick back and enjoy a delicious meal, a beautiful sunset, a great party, or a long laugh.

On a sabbatical I had the opportunity to go to Italy with my family. We were on one of those tour buses where the guide offers a constant flow of interesting facts over the microphone, but because of jetlag and information overload, my mind wasn't absorbing them all. Somewhere in the busy succession of famous sites and important landmarks, he turned and told the driver to stop. Then he pointed out a gorgeous landscape on the left and a beautiful cityscape on the right. The rest of that day, every scene seemed more remarkable and amazing. Stopping and noticing the wonder of my surroundings completely changed my perspective.

I think God wants us to stop sometimes, look to the right and the left, and notice that it's a beautiful life full of blessings like spouses, children, parents, friends, wonderful meals, fascinating landscapes, and awe-inspiring skies. Even when life isn't going the way we want it to, we can still find God's gifts around us if we'll open our eyes to them.

Ancient Israel celebrated many occasions with a party: the weaning of a child, a king's birthday, the arrival of a dignitary, the departure of a dignitary, sheep shearing—almost any occasion was worth celebrating, many with an all-out feast. For weddings, everyone took a week off and partied for seven days. And these were just the private feasts. Communal feasts were widespread and included the new moon each month, Sabbaths, and all of the national feasts specified in the law. They were appointed by God so his people would never forget how he had worked in their lives. He set apart times for worship, rest, the reading of his Word, and sharing food. Even the serious and somber feasts were followed by as much as a week of singing, dancing, and eating. The Hebrew calendar had far more holidays on it than ours ever has.

The New Testament has its share of happiness too. When Jesus said, "Blessed are the poor in spirit, . . . those who mourn, . . . the meek," and so on, the word for *blessed* actually means "happy" and "fortunate" (Matt. 5:3–12). His point in the Beatitudes was not to inform us of our obligations but of the way to be happy. He also backed up that message with his works. His first recorded miracle wasn't a healing or a deliverance. He turned water into wine at a wedding—a weeklong feast that included dancing, eating, and drinking. The jars he filled with wine were huge; they would make a keg look small. And the guests thought it was better wine than they had been drinking all week. A miracle to save face for the hosts and prolong a party might seem a little frivolous to some of us—it might even violate some of our traditions—but that's because we assume Jesus always had a serious look on his face as the movies portray. According to the Bible, though, he knew how to have a good time, and he encouraged others to do the same.

The early church transformed the world, and joy was one of the main reasons. Someone has said that *love* was the early Christians' marketing plan and their business card was *joy*. In spite of difficult circumstances and persecution, in the midst of the fallenness of life, early believers richly drank in the good things of God, enjoyed fellowship with each other, often over shared meals, and greeted each other with "a holy kiss"—a warm embrace (Rom. 16:16). They took great risks, made great sacrifices, prayed great prayers, and dreamed great dreams. But they also had a lot of fun.

The New Testament actually commands us to enjoy great moments. The first part of this verse is familiar to many: "Instruct those who are rich in this present world not to be conceited or to fix their hope on the uncertainty of riches" (1 Tim. 6:17 NASB). But the rest of the verse is often overlooked as though it's a footnote on the main point, even though the command can't be truly understood without the follow-up phrase. The "do not" about fixing hope on riches has a corresponding "do this instead." Paul says that their focus should be on God, "who richly supplies us with *all things to enjoy*" (v. 17 NASB, emphasis added). That's relatively clear. God gives us things for our pleasure. Enjoying life is definitely allowed. It's even part of God's game plan to protect us from our arch enemy, materialism.

Unwillingness to Face False Beliefs and Unhealthy Behavior

Why is it so easy for us to grasp the prohibitions of Scripture and so hard to remember the privileges? Because all of us struggle with false beliefs and unhealthy behaviors that come from a distorted view of God and a warped theology of pleasure. If we want to get past them, we have to face them. Otherwise we'll keep going down unhealthy paths trying to find joy and happiness from something or someone that can't and won't deliver.

Which behaviors or attitudes may be thwarting God's desire for you to enjoy him and the great moments he has provided for you? Do you have workaholic tendencies, for example? If you find your identity in what you do, you're likely to spend long hours establishing, improving, and defending that identity. Or if you're a perfectionist, the drive to make every task flawless will consume your life. If your significance depends on doing everything right, your job never ends. Or maybe you tend to seek approval by saying *yes* to everyone who asks you to do something. Then you end up with plenty of friends who virtually own all of your time. Human beings have no shortage of flawed motives driving us to keep piling busyness on ourselves and forfeiting the call of God to enjoy the life he gives us. Some immerse ourselves in work as a means of escape, while others—quite a few of us, in fact—use it to support a materialistic lifestyle that keeps us always running but never arriving.

All of these tendencies are performance-oriented distortions of the truth. They keep us running on a treadmill, always pursuing but never arriving. I've always struggled with the lie that I can enjoy life, spend time with the family, and do the things that really recharge me only after I've gotten all my work done. That's the Protestant work ethic, isn't it? Figuratively and literally, you can't eat dessert until you've eaten all your vegetables. The only problem—at least with life, if not with food—is that the vegetables never end. If I wait until all my work is done to relax and be restored, I'll be perpetually stressed because the work is never done. The discipline of finishing work before having fun is great for a school kid—I'm grateful for that early training—but it can be so embedded in an adult psyche like mine that it becomes an obsession rather than a good habit.

Enjoyable, renewing activities are the key to healing and effectiveness in leadership. A performance-based life eats away at health and sanity. It creates guilt whenever the goals of perfection, approval, and maximum production are not fully reached—which means it always produces guilt. If you feel guilty having fun, maybe it will help to remember that enjoying the richness of God's gifts is a command. *Not* to enjoy life is actually disobedient! As C. S. Lewis said, "Joy is the serious business of heaven."

Get Serious About Having Fun

It's one thing to understand why it's permissible to enjoy life. It's another to actually start doing it. For some people, that comes naturally. Most of us, however, have to retrain ourselves to leave bad habits behind and establish healthy attitudes and behaviors. I've found the following practices helpful in my efforts to overcome my workaholic, perfectionist tendencies and enjoy great moments.

Slow Down

A friend gave this advice to pastor and author John Ortberg: "Ruthlessly eliminate hurry from your life."[4] Speed kills joy. Many of us are multitaskers who feel good when we get seven things done at the same time. About ten years ago, I read a book by the same friend who gave that advice (Dallas Willard), and he said spiritual development and intimacy with God are impossible in a hurried life.[5] That gave me plenty of incentive to change, but it took a consistent, conscious effort to slow down. For about two years, unless circumstances were completely unavoidable, I drove in the right lane on the freeway, chose the longest line at the grocery store, and got to meetings ten minutes early. Eventually it dawned on me that underneath all of my habitual hurry was a kind of arrogance that convinced me wherever I was going was more important than where everyone else was going. That's why I always needed to be at the front of the line or in the fastest lane. That attitude doesn't go over well with God; he's always opposed to the proud. That's why he says, "Be still, and know that I am God" (Ps. 46:10). It's important to humble ourselves, take a deep breath, and slow down. God will accomplish all of his purposes even when you stop and do nothing for a season to enjoy a great moment.

Slim Down

This isn't a weight-loss plan—not literally, anyway. Slim down in other areas of your life: Simplify your schedule, your meals, your commitments, your goals—whatever needs simplifying. Don't let yourself get overextended. Examine some of the things you're doing and ask whether you really need to be doing them. Realize that your priority in life should be a relationship *with* Christ, not an agenda *for* him. The classic example of this in Scripture is the well-known story of Mary and Martha in Luke 10:38–42. Mary sat at the feet of Jesus while Martha was busy being a good hostess. Jesus praised Mary for realizing what was most important at the time: simply being with him.

I made a decision years ago that some would consider almost heretical. I looked at all the time and energy that went into sending Christmas cards and decided not to do them anymore. I realized that sending them wasn't required by law. People who don't get one from me know that I love them; they just know I don't do cards. Are greeting cards wrong? Of course not. But for me at that time, that was a decision that greatly simplified life. I share that story not to slam the tradition of Christmas cards or hurt Hallmark's sales. The point is that sometimes you need to stop and question the activities, traditions, *ought*s, and *should*s in your life. The demands of life constantly force us to add new things to our schedule. Why not consider asking God where you need to subtract a few?

Sit Down

Learn to live in the present. Most of us either live *for* tomorrow or live *because of* yesterday. Our focus is on the future or the past, and we never really get to enjoy the present. First Thessalonians 5:16–18 says, "Rejoice always [present tense]; pray without ceasing [present tense]; in everything give thanks [present tense]; for this is God's will for you in Christ Jesus" (NASB). Life will become a lot more enjoyable when we take stock, focus on what we have rather than what we don't have, drink it all in, and thank him.

Think about how much of our activity is based on all the things we have to do to get the future we want—or on proving that the person who years ago said we'd never amount to anything was wrong. We can't really control either the past or the future, but when we try to live in either direction, we miss the present—the only time we really ever have. As a mentor once told me, "Chip, follow your great impulses." So live today! Enjoy this moment.

Look Around

What blessing from God can you celebrate today? Especially look at the little things you often take for granted. For over twelve years I lived a mile and a half from the ocean, and at one point I realized that I'd gone about nine months without having seen it. So I made myself get up early on Sunday mornings, park on a cliff overlooking the Pacific, watch the waves come in and the sun come up, and thank God for all the beauty he created. Recently, I've started leaving the house early in the morning when it's still dark, and I've noticed something I'd never seen before: a huge star that looks awesome against the black sky. On one occasion I pulled into my driveway and saw a hawk in a bush next to my house, and for some reason it didn't fly away. I had things to do, calls to make, and people to see, but I thought, "When am I ever going to be six feet away from a hawk again?" So I just sat in my car and looked at him, thinking about how his eye could probably see a mouse from a couple hundred feet in the air. It's not natural for me, or for most people, to pause and reflect on the beauty and enormity of creation. We have to be intentional about drinking it all in.

Plan In

Schedule great moments into your daily, weekly, monthly, and annual calendar. The only way I've been able to have a regular date with my wife, enjoy a cup of coffee in the morning, have some personal worship time, and create meaningful moments like that is by planning them into my schedule. Otherwise, it's a matter of grabbing some coffee on the way out the door, picking up a quick lunch at a drive-thru window, running red lights to get to work on time, and living with high blood pressure. There's no way to have a joyful, winsome testimony with a lifestyle like that. Christians who are able to plan into their schedule fun activities, time with family and friends, one-minute "vacations," or a leisurely walk through the woods are going to have a much closer relationship with God.

That's what it's all about. There's no way to become great without maintaining the vitality of that relationship. Anyone who wants to be a great Christian has to have great fellowship with Christ. And anyone who wants to have great fellowship with him has to make it a priority to enjoy great moments.

Action Steps

1. One day this week, go to a park for lunch and watch some kids play on a playground. On another day, try listening to some awesome music with your eyes closed for ten minutes. Look around, drink life in, and enjoy the beauty God has placed around you.
2. Think of a friend, coworker, or family member who needs some encouragement, and then take the time this week to provide it. Have lunch or a cup of coffee with that person,

call just to say hello, or send a card to let that person know you're thinking of him or her.

3. Memorize Proverbs 17:22, "A cheerful heart is good medicine, but a crushed spirit dries up the bones."

Questions for Reflection and Discussion

1. If someone asked the people who know you best if you are a happy person who really enjoys life, how do you think they would answer? What evidence would they give for their answer?

2. Of the tendencies identified on page 179 (workaholism, perfectionism, approval seeking, escapism, and materialism), which is most likely to keep you from enjoying God and the great moments he has planned for you? What can you do to overcome that tendency?

3. What is your reaction to the thought of early believers having fun with each other? Does that make them seem more or less spiritual? Why?

9

Empower Great People

It's a familiar scene. Two boys on the playground get into an argument, which soon turns into a scuffle. But scuffles on playgrounds usually don't settle much, especially when adults intervene and separate the combatants. The verbal contest continues until they both wield the same ultimate taunt: "My dad can beat up your dad." That's the highest they can go in the pecking order of power. They're trying to answer the question of who's the best.

We have plenty of adult ways to ask the same question. Every professional sports league crowns a champion, and nearly every one names a "Most Valuable Player." *Forbes* magazine measures greatness by dollar signs and market share. *People* magazine measures greatness by popularity and good looks. Our culture has awards for best dressed, best tasting, world's greatest, world's fastest, world's sexiest, most likely to succeed, person of the year—you get the point. Commentators on sports talk shows debate whether a certain team from 1960-something could beat a certain team from 1980-something or whether a big-name boxer from the 1940s could outduel a big-name boxer of today. Those debates go on to bestowing titles such as "world's greatest" or "best of all time." Deep inside us is a competitive drive that finds innumerable ways to compare and climb higher. And the fundamental question behind that drive, the question that every human being asks until the day he or she dies, is, "Who's the greatest?"

Jesus's disciples certainly asked that question. After three years of walking with him, seeing the world's greatest miracles, and hearing the world's greatest sermons, they brought up a concern that was on their heart. James and John, two of Jesus's closest friends, knew he was about to come into his kingdom. They didn't quite understand the nature of his kingdom yet, thinking he would free Israel from Rome and establish his own throne. So they asked if one of them could sit on his left and the other on his right. Plain and simple, they wanted to be famous, to be respected, and to have powerful positions. They wanted to be acknowledged as great.

That was a rather bold request. It was nervy enough that the other disciples got really bent out of shape about it—probably not because they thought it was a bad idea, but because James and John had the guts to ask him first. And Jesus responded with a radical redefinition of greatness. He called them together and laid it all out for them.

First, he pointed out that the request of James and John matched the world's definition of greatness perfectly—and it was a bad definition. They were not to fit that mold. Then he gave them the godly alternative: "Whoever wants to become great among you must be your servant, and whoever wants to be first must be slave of all" (Mark 10:43–44). What would that look like in real life? Jesus used himself as the prime example: "Even the Son of Man did not come to be served, but to serve, and to give his life as a ransom for many" (v. 45).

I think it's rather amazing that Jesus didn't reprove James and John for asking the question, and he didn't reprove the other ten for being indignant. This wasn't the only time this issue came up—I referred to a similar episode from Luke 22 in the introduction—and each time Jesus dealt with it consistently. Instead of chastising his friends, he pulled them all together and, in effect, affirmed the desire to be great. He focused not on their goal but on the means to get there. In the eyes of people, you have to have power, prestige, beauty, and wealth to be considered great. But in God's eyes? The lower you go, the better. You have to be the servant of all.

True greatness is serving others for the glory of God. In a nutshell, that's the way to higher standing in God's kingdom. We take our eyes off of ourselves and turn them to God and others. We become great in God's eyes by helping others become greater than ourselves.

I had been studying and teaching this topic for a couple of years when I received a book in the mail, completely out of the blue. I think it was from someone I had met at a convention. Its title immediately caught my attention: *Humility: True Greatness*. Since I had been so immersed in the issue of greatness in God's eyes, receiving this book seemed like a God-orchestrated "coincidence." As I read through it, I came across this statement:

> In each of our lives, if we're going to have any possibility of becoming truly great in God's eyes, it means turning upside down the entrenched worldly ideas of our definition of greatness. The difference couldn't be more stark, as sinfully and culturally defined greatness looks like this: individuals motivated by self-interest, self-indulgence, and a false sense of self-sufficiency, pursue selfish ambition for the purpose of self-glorification. . . . Serving others for the glory of God; this is the genuine expression of humility. This is true greatness as our Savior defines it.[1]

Great Christians Empower Great People

Greatness comes through building others up, by aiming for their greatness more than we aim for our own. That competitive drive we all have tells us that our gain is someone else's loss, and someone else's loss is our gain. Not so in the kingdom of God, where the logic of human minds is turned upside down and inside out. In God's economy, someone else's gain is our gain, and someone else's loss is our loss. The best way to greatness in an economy like that is to pursue greatness—for someone else.

Paul put it this way to Timothy: "The things you have heard me say in the presence of many witnesses entrust to reliable men who will also be qualified to teach others" (2 Tim. 2:2). Paul had invested himself in Timothy and wanted Timothy to become a great pastor. So what does he tell him to do? Equip others. Our ultimate service to others is to help them become all God intends for them to be. Great Christians empower great people.

Paul's instructions to Timothy show four generations of personal investment in others. Paul served Timothy, Timothy was to serve a select group of faithful people who had a heart for God, and these people were to be equipped to serve others. Each generation enhanced its own greatness by focusing on the next generation.

We see this dynamic often in Scripture. Moses is considered the greatest of all Old Testament leaders, but among all of his other major responsibilities, he took the time to train his successor. So Moses gave the law, but Joshua actually led God's people into the Promised Land. Eli mentored Samuel for years, and Samuel had far more impact on the people of Israel. Elijah is known as the prophetic prototype, yet his apprentice, Elisha, boldly asked for a double portion of Elijah's spirit and ended up doing exactly twice as many miracles as the older prophet.

John the Baptist, an Elijah-like prophet, is considered a bridge between the Old and New Testaments, and his attitude is a perfect example of the servant heart Jesus taught his disciples. At one point in John's ministry, his disciples were concerned that his popularity was declining while Jesus's was rising. John responded with a classic statement of selflessness: "He must increase, but I must decrease" (John 3:30 NASB). What did Jesus think of this kind of attitude? Even if we may not know for sure, Jesus later said, "Among those born of women there is no one greater than John" (Luke 7:28). In the kingdom of God, decreasing equals greatness.

More than anyone else in the Bible—or in history, for that matter—Jesus had a right to focus exclusively on his own greatness. But he spent three years empowering twelve men who, along with the generations they in turn empowered, reached most of the known world with the gospel.

While Paul's investment in Timothy is one of the clearest examples in the early church of empowering great people, he gave up on another. John Mark had bailed out on Paul's first missionary journey, and the apostle didn't want him coming along the next time. But Barnabas saw potential in spite of the younger missionary's failure and took the time to mentor him—effectively enough that Paul was able to say later in his life that John Mark was of great use to him (Acts 15:36–41; 2 Tim. 4:11).

Good Christians live the Christian life. They love God, walk in integrity, demonstrate faithfulness to their mates, spend time in the Bible because they want to hear from God, make the effort to discover their spiritual gifts, use those gifts in their local church, give their tithes and offerings, go on mission trips, and help their kids grow up to be godly men and women. They do what God calls them to do, and they serve him well.

> **Good Christians "live the life"; great Christians "leave a legacy."**

Great Christians, on the other hand, do all that and then pass it on. You can be a good Christian by obeying God and loving people, but if you haven't poured your life into others, your life ends with a period. Great Christians end with a comma. They live the life of faith in a way that takes God's grace to them and imparts it into the lives of others. They multiply themselves again and again and again. Good Christians "live the life"; great Christians "leave a legacy."

How to Leave a Legacy for God's Glory

Edward Kimball taught Sunday school in Boston in the 1850s, and one of his students, a reluctant church member, weighed heavily on his heart for months. The student was spiritually dense and unable to understand biblical concepts, Kimball later said. But the teacher stuck with the teenager and won his friendship

with kindness. He encouraged him, an uneducated shoe sales-
man, to keep attending church and studying the Bible. One day
he visited his student at work and nervously shared the gospel
with him, and the young man accepted Christ. The mentoring
relationship continued as the two became lifelong friends. Kimball was simply one ordinary man who invested part of his life
in an ordinary kid who seemed to need some guidance.

Those are the kinds of relationships God uses to build his
kingdom. The young man Kimball took an interest in was
Dwight Moody, whose later ministry won hundreds of thousands of people to Christ, who founded a Bible institute that
has prepared thousands to live a life of influence, and whose
legacy continues to impact millions today. As far as I know,
Kimball isn't known for leading anyone but Moody to Christ
or for mentoring any other younger men, at least not in sub-
stantial numbers, but in the kingdom of heaven, he shares
the same reward as his more famous pupil. Moody's legacy is
Kimball's legacy—all because one ordinary person reproduced
his relationship with God in the life of another.

Dawson Trotman, founder of the Navigators, said, "Activity
is no substitute for productivity; productivity is no substitute
for reproduction."[2] A lot of Christians are very active doing a
lot of things and attending a lot of meetings. Many of them are
actually quite productive. They bear fruit. But few Christians
are reproducing their life—leaving a legacy by developing a
spiritual lineage. If you want to empower great people, how,
practically, can you do it?

Help Many, Train a Few

You have to invest wisely. One principle drawn from 2 Timothy 2:2 is to help a lot of people but train only a few. You can
contribute to the lives of many, but you can't invest deeply in
everyone. You have to choose. The key to Jesus's impact was
selection. He helped the multitudes, but he trained a few who
would change the world. That raises a critical question: How
do you know whom to invest your life in?

Pray

The first step in that direction is to pray. James 1:5 says that if anyone lacks wisdom—if you realize that you don't know how to live life skillfully and to do what God has called you to do—then ask God, "who gives generously to all without finding fault." We have plenty of scriptural examples of people who left a great legacy—Moses, Elijah, Jesus, Paul, to name a few—and invariably they were people of great prayer. We forget that godly wisdom is there for the asking. It only makes sense that we would begin by saying, "Lord, I want to focus and invest my life in a few people, so I need to be discerning. Please guide me in this." And God, who is more interested in your becoming a great Christian than even you are, has promised to answer.

Look Under Your Own Roof

Empowering great people starts with those for whom you are morally responsible. In 1 Timothy 3:4, Paul says that a leader "must manage his own family well and see that his children obey him with proper respect." Many pastors' and missionaries' kids grow up so rebellious and undisciplined that you have to wonder if their parents were so busy helping others that they had no idea what was going on at home. The attributes required to be successful in business—and, by worldly standards, even in ministry—are the very attributes least conducive to a healthy home life. That's why studies of the top executives have a much higher rate of kids and spouses who struggle with depression, addiction, and suicide. Only the very poor have a worse track record.[3] If you want to be the kind of Christian—rich, poor, professional, or unemployed—who empowers great people, begin with those who live with you.

I watched my wife model this principle. About ten years ago, she got out of her comfort zone and spoke in front of three hundred women. She received an amazing response, and part of her message was aired on our radio program. She soon received numerous invitations to speak at churches around the country. I assured her that I'd be fine staying at home with the kids while she explored this area of ministry, but she refused.

"Chip," she said, "I can go speak at these events to encourage women and sprinkle a little bit of grace here and there. But when we get to heaven, our greatest impact will not be on the people for whom I add a sixteenth of an inch to their spiritual depth. Our greatest impact will be on our kids. If God wants me to do this when they get older, fine. But for now, these kids are my ministry."

She was right. The time and energy we invested in the spiritual growth of our children has paid huge dividends in their lives and ministries. We had a strategic plan to build into our kids the things that really matter. My wife's focus and boundaries helped us stay on track in leaving the most important legacy we could leave.

Look for F.A.T. People

After praying and looking under your own roof, look for F.A.T. people. No offense intended; that has nothing to do with body weight and everything to do with the characteristics of a person worth investing in: Faithful, Available, and Teachable.

Proverbs 20:6 says, "Many a man claims to have unfailing love, but a faithful man who can find?" *Faithful* people are the ones who complete an assignment, who actually take care of a problem when they say they'll take care of it, and who call you later because they promised they would. We get all wrapped up in the potential people seem to have based on their personality and talents, but God doesn't. He looks at the heart. Those who are faithful have put themselves in a position to grow in maturity. Instead of listening to what people say, watch what they do with their responsibilities. When you see faithfulness, you see potential.

Faithfulness alone isn't enough, however. Someone can be very faithful and yet be pointed in twenty different directions. They'll say, "I want to grow, I want to learn, let's get together," but then be out of town every other week. There's nothing wrong with that, but they aren't going to be a high-yield spiritual investment. To invest your life wisely, you'll want to choose people who are *available* in addition to being faithful.

Look also for people who are *teachable*. A person who thinks he or she has already mastered certain aspects of life is not going to be open to instruction or even subtle suggestions. There's no point in investing in someone who isn't aware that the investment is beneficial. People who are teachable are in position to grow and bear fruit.

You discover whether people are teachable by how they respond when confronted with hard things to hear. Do they hear constructive criticism with humility? Do they respond with character and demonstrate surrender and perseverance? There's a real danger in evaluating people the way the world does. We often fall into the trap of seeing people who have a sharp mind, a great personality, and the right education as those who are most likely to make an impact for Christ. But God chooses the lowly things of this world in order to shame our worldly standards (1 Cor. 1:27–29). In the New Testament he used former prostitutes, homosexuals, idol worshipers, thieves, and drunkards by redeeming them and giving them spiritual gifts to use for the benefit of others. I encourage you to look beyond people's history and look at their heart. If they happen to be "sharp," fine. But resist making that your unconscious criteria. If they are faithful, available, and teachable, they can become who God really wants them to be.

When I first moved to Santa Cruz, I didn't know much about leadership, but I could still see that there wasn't much structure in that church of eight or nine hundred people. There was vast potential, but no organization can grow unless you increase the base (see figure on next page). So our leadership set out to discover who our latent leaders were in order to invest in them first before starting new programs or strategies. We weren't necessarily looking for the best intellects and charismatic personalities. We wanted to find the top fifty potential lay leaders in the church—ordinary people from all walks of life—who were faithful, available, and teachable and then pour our lives into them. Then they would become the mentors who would invest their lives in others.

The only way to get a larger pyramid
is to expand the base—in this case, leadership.

We had a "draft day" when each staff member and elder picked several leadership candidates and invited each one into a process. We would get them in a Bible study for eight weeks, learn about their lives, and convey to them the vision of the church. But we had one rule: every group had to start before 6:30 in the morning. Why? For one thing, I knew no one would have a scheduling conflict then. But more significantly, there's no better way to find out if someone is faithful, available, and teachable than by asking him or her to commit to an important but inconvenient endeavor. Humility, surrender, and consistency—or the lack thereof—show up in such situations. You discover who's really in the game and who isn't.

Forty-five of our top fifty potential leaders signed up, and three years later we could look back and see a major transformation in the lives of our individual members and the life of our church. Most people want to be challenged, not just on their gifts, reputation, or financial capacity, but on their commitment to the cause. They want to grow and learn. Those who *really* want to, not just with good intentions but by putting feet to their faith, will rise to the challenge and grow to the next level of discipleship. Those are the people you want to invest in because they will take the investment and multiply it in the next generation. They will leave a legacy for God's glory.

The Jesus School of Empowering Others

If it's God's desire for us to leave a legacy, it only makes sense that we would be able to see the practice modeled in Jesus's ministry. We know about the legacy he left. Even unbelievers know about this one man who never traveled farther than sixty miles from his home and who had no mass media exposure. Eleven of his twelve closest followers were very committed, and a hundred and twenty others were more loosely committed. Two thousand years later we acknowledge his importance every time we write the date on a check. He's the dividing line in history because of the power of his life—and because he passed his life on to others, who in turn passed it on to others, and so on. How did he do that?

Jesus had a fourfold process of empowering great people that stands out clearly in the Gospels. He *brought them in, built them up, trained them for action*, and *sent them out*. His disciples were ordinary people, mostly blue-collar workers, who were faithful, available, and teachable. Regular people like them—and like us—can follow the fourfold process of the greatest person ever to live in order to leave a lasting legacy for God's glory.

1. Bring Them In

The key to drawing people into the kind of relationship in which you can serve and empower them is *exposure*. You first have to model the message. Then you can invite them into the action and engage them in authentic relationships. Mark 3:14 says that Jesus appointed twelve men and designated them apostles (messengers, or "sent ones"), "that they might be with him." His methodology was very simple; he just wanted them to be around him.

That's what Dave Marshall, the mentor I mentioned in chapter 3, did for me. He had only a high school education and wasn't very "cool" by my young college standards, but he loved me and knew the Bible better than I did, and he still does. He came alongside me and taught me how to study the Bible, helped me memorize verses, showed me how to share my faith, and modeled how a Christian does marriage and family. I learned from him through heart-to-heart talks and watching how he lived. I was discipled simply by hanging out with him and catching his values and authenticity. He brought me in by modeling the message, inviting me to participate, and engaging me in genuine relationship.

Very often we want to speed up the process by getting people involved in activity and giving them a few books to read and messages to listen to. That may provide the information they need, but it doesn't give them any pictures of what the Christian life should look like. Jesus's method of discipleship was to live with his disciples. That's it. They went where he went, heard what he said, saw what he did, ate what he ate, and talked with him about everyday matters. When we engage people like that, we bring them in. They need to smell and taste and see the winsome life of Christ in us before anything else.

2. Build Them Up

Jesus told his disciples that if they followed him, he would make them fishers of men (Matt. 4:19). That goes beyond exposing them to his life and message; it moves into a stage of *nurture*. Jesus affirmed their strengths, inspired their dreams, and confronted their flaws.

Even when I had no Bible training, Dave encouraged me to trust insights I had into the text. He even asked me to lead the Bible study sometimes. His teaching wasn't necessarily very charismatic—I listened to tapes he gave me three years later and told him how awesome the message was, and he reminded me that I slept through it the first time—but our small group went from about 6 students to 250 in personal Bible study around our campus. All along the way, he affirmed and cultivated the teaching gift he saw developing in me. After each session I led, we'd have coffee and he'd point out what I had done well. Then he'd slip in a few suggestions that would make it better next time, but he was never harsh or critical. He didn't dwell on my weaknesses, and he affirmed my strengths.

After seminary, I pastored a small church outside of Dallas. I was very encouraged to see the congregation grow from about 35 people to 500 in roughly seven years. But I had a gnawing feeling of dissatisfaction and finally expressed it to Don, a pastor who had mentored me during my seminary days.

"We're in a county of four thousand people and there are about eighteen churches within two miles of here," I lamented. "If people want to hear the gospel in rural Texas, they can. I love these folks, but I came to seminary to be a missionary, and I feel like I'm just scratching the surface. I want to pastor a large church in a cutting-edge place. Is that wrong?"

We hesitate to voice a dream like that out loud because it sounds a little arrogant. People might think we're on an ego trip and only interested in doing *big* things. But *big* wasn't my motivation; impact was.

"Chip," Don said, "you know pastors of large churches aren't any better than pastors of small churches, right?"

"Yes, I know."

"It's just a difference in gifts, and there's a certain gift mix needed in a larger church. It's hard to find that mix. People call me all the time from all over the country about vacancies in large churches needing a pastor. Pray about your motives, but if God has put that on your heart, you ought to be open to it."

About a year later, Santa Cruz Bible Church called me. It's a large church in an area with relatively little Christian influence. All I needed was someone to tell me that it was okay to dream a dream. In the same way, most of the people we mentor feel like they need permission to think outside the box. Part of empowering great people is inspiring their dreams.

Yet you also need to be able to confront their flaws. Dave affirmed my strengths, and Don inspired me to dream, but when I think of confrontation, I think of Jerry. Jerry was a layman who loved college kids, so he worked full time and spent his remaining hours discipling students. One day he said to me, "Let's have breakfast tomorrow," which, in the lingo of our fellowship, was code language for, "We need to talk about something rather heavy." About halfway through my Egg McMuffin, Jerry opened his Bible to Proverbs 27:5–6 and read it to me: "Better is open rebuke than hidden love. Wounds from a friend can be trusted, but an enemy multiplies kisses." In other words, "I love you enough to say some things that will really hurt." Then Jerry looked me in the eye and told me that I came across as arrogant, that my mouth kept getting me in trouble, that I was self-focused, and that I always tried to put myself at the center of attention.

"Chip," he continued, "when I was riding with you the other day, you acted like you were the most important person on the highway and the laws were just for other people." And item by item, he listed evidence of pride in my life.

Can you guess what my first reaction was? It certainly wasn't, "Thank you, brother. You must really love me to be so honest with me." I was offended and not very open to what he had to say. But after my initial offense, I heeded his words, and as I look back, the few people who bluntly confronted me with my own issues are the people I most appreciate now. They were right. I *was* arrogant and mouthy, and what comes out of the mouth *is* a true expression of what's in someone's heart. When they questioned whether I could glorify God while I was so busy seeking to please and impress people, they were right on target. They went for the jugular, straight to the character issues coming out of my heart. They loved me enough to confront me. As a result, they produced in me the practice of "speaking the truth in love" with other people close to me. As my kids were growing up, they knew that any time Dad wanted to talk about something serious, there was one line they were sure to hear: "Guys, this is a spiritual issue." I passed that on to them because Jerry and a few others passed it on to me.

3. Train Them for Action

Training is about *structure*. Jesus told his disciples that "a student is not above his teacher, but everyone who is fully trained will be like his teacher" (Luke 6:40). When you fully train someone, whether it's a child, a student, or a friend, that person is going to be a lot like you. So in the structure phase of empowering great people, we need to instruct their minds, develop their hearts, and equip their hands.

God used many laypeople and pastors to provide this in my life over the years, but Howard Hendricks played a particularly big role. I related my experience in chapter 3 of a relationship that began with him as my professor and has continued with him as my mentor. I took every course he taught and listened to everything he's ever spoken about. For some reason, God gave me a sense of connection with him that has shaped how I think biblically about discipleship, relationships, money, preaching, confrontation, and life in general. "Prof," as his students call him, understood that he was not only training my head but also developing my heart and equipping my hands for ministry.

I'll never forget Bill Lawrence, another mentor who helped equip me. I was in a leadership evaluation program in which experts looked at your preaching, your family, and your ministry under a microscope. They even interviewed a lot of people who knew you all too well—it was very thorough. At one point during this process, Bill sat down with Theresa and me to watch a couple of my preaching videos. I knew Bill well enough to know he cared deeply about me, so the context was within an established relationship. But I still wasn't prepared for what he said.

"Chip, I just can't figure out the real issue here. I don't know whether you're just plain lazy or you don't believe in preaching."

I was stunned. My wife was in the room, and my immediate thought was, "What are you doing? Real men don't do this to real men!" And where did he get off saying that anyway? I was growing a little church into something bigger and had a discipleship mind-set. For sermon preparation, I studied the text enough to be comfortable talking about it in front of the congregation. I didn't do that last 15 percent of the hard work of preaching we were taught to do—writing out the transitions and illustrations. But real life-change happens in small groups anyway, and I was spending seventy or eighty hours a week majoring on that. I got quite angry initially and let Bill know I didn't think he was on target.

"Laziness isn't being inactive," he said. "Laziness is not doing the right thing at the right time to fulfill the right assignment. You're gifted enough that all those people in that small town think you're pretty good, don't they?"

"Yeah, I guess so."

"And you think you're pretty good too, don't you?"

"Yeah, pretty good."

"Well, you're not as good as you think. Some preaching is like a flashlight. It spreads light and everybody gets a little glimpse of it. Other preaching is like a laser beam. It can cut through a steel door. Your problem is focus. That last 15 percent of a great message is very hard work, and you're not doing it. God has given you a significant communication gift, and you're going to stand before the judgment seat of Christ to give an accounting for it. Life-change does happen in small groups, but it's not an either-or proposition. You are to be the best communicator you can be for Christ. You'd better figure that out, and you'd better give your best effort to preaching."

Then my wife piped up—in love, of course. "Well, I don't know that he's lazy; he does a lot of work. But it's true that he doesn't believe in preaching."

From that point on, I blocked off the first two hours of every day after my time with God, and all of Wednesday until noon, to work on messages. I focused on that last 15 percent that changes a message from a flashlight to a laser. Do I think less of Bill today for that difficult training period? Not a chance. In fact, I got a video from him six weeks ago, put it in the player, and thought as I watched it about how God used him to change my life twenty years ago.

Not everyone will need equipping in pastoral skills like that, but everyone must learn certain skills in the Christian life before going further: how to study the Bible, how to manage finances, how to articulate your faith, how to handle relationship conflict, and so on. Empowering great people requires specific training in specific areas.

4. Send Them Out

Finally comes the *challenge* stage. Jesus sent his disciples on a mission. The early missions were small, very specific, and followed by times of debriefing, encouragement, and evaluation (Luke 10:1–24). After they experienced success and had learned to trust Jesus's presence and promises, he *sent them forth* to fulfill his eternal plan for humanity. "Go and make disciples of all nations, baptizing them in the name of the Father and of the Son and of the Holy Spirit, and teaching them to obey everything I have commanded you" (Matt. 28:19–20). And he followed it up with a promise that the mentoring would continue. He would be with them always.

When you send someone out, you have to clarify the mission ("This is what I want you to do"), confirm their calling ("I'm on your side; I know you can do this"), and continue to mentor. You help people understand how God made them and called them. When they step out in faith, they're going to get some opposition, so you continue to stand by them to help them through difficult seasons.

This is why God made the body of Christ to be dependent on him and interdependent on one another. There are no superstars in his kingdom. Some people have gifts that make them more visible, but everyone has an opportunity to leave a legacy. Our goal, whether it's with our children or our successors, is to help them become great. When I go back to the church in Santa Cruz, I'm amazed at the pastors and key leaders who are now leading ministries or who are now pastoring their own churches far better than I did. When I look at my kids, I'm amazed at the potential they have to reach farther and higher than I ever hope to. Empowering great people is about letting your ceiling become the next generation's floor. You equip them to start where you leave off and build on it.

Why Do So Few Leave a Legacy?

Leaving a legacy of continuing and lasting fruitfulness is possible for any and every Christ follower. So why do so many of us fail in this arena? Prof Hendricks offers three reasons: lack of discipline, lack of vision, and lack of focus.

Lack of Discipline

We cannot impart what we do not possess. One of the reasons for Paul's lasting legacy was his ability to tell people, with all integrity, to follow his example. "Therefore I urge you to imitate me. For this reason I am sending to you Timothy, my son whom I love, who is faithful in the Lord. He will remind you of my way of life in Christ Jesus, which agrees with what I teach everywhere in every church" (1 Cor. 4:16–17). That's like telling your kids, "Drive how I drive; spend how I spend; manage your time like I manage mine; love your wife like I love your mother." That's challenging, and it requires discipline.

You can't issue that kind of challenge to your family or those you are discipling unless you mean it. If you ask yourself, "Am I sure I want the people I influence to imitate me?" and wonder whether that's a good idea, do what it takes to become exemplary. It may require turning off the TV, kicking an old habit, or getting up a little earlier. But if it really matters to you, you'll do it.

Lack of Vision

"Our failure to see beyond our own life span is a real hindrance," Prof Hendricks once said. I tried making a list of some of the people Prof has mentored over the years and was easily able to come up with about ten of today's most well-known, productive leaders and communicators in ministry. Prof hasn't focused on building a media ministry, writing tons of books, or pastoring a series of enormous churches, but a lot of the people who are doing those things can point directly to his influence. I'm glad he had the vision to invest in Chuck Swindoll, Joe Stowell, David Jeremiah, Tony Evans, Dennis Rainey, and a host of others. As a seminary professor, he saw beyond his own lifetime and is leaving a massive legacy. Every unnoticed

Sunday school teacher or small-group leader who understands the importance of watering spiritual seeds is doing the same.

Lack of Focus

Prof often said that "a life of impact is about the *one* thing I do, not the twenty things I dabble in." That sounds a lot like Paul's words to the Philippians:

> One thing I do: Forgetting what is behind and straining toward what is ahead, I press on toward the goal to win the prize for which God has called me heavenward in Christ Jesus.
> All of us who are mature should take such a view of things. And if on some point you think differently, that too God will make clear to you.
>
> Philippians 3:13–15

Lasting legacies flow out of single-minded and wholehearted focus. You can spread yourself thin by trying to help everyone all the time and end up wondering how your life slipped away. Or you can help many and train a few. It takes focus.

God promises great things for those who bear fruit that lasts. The only way to do that is to empower others. Inspire them to greatness and help them get there. Serve them by setting them up with the tools to exceed your own impact. The world has been radically affected by a Savior who practiced that principle and taught his followers to do the same. Your greatness as a Christian is fundamentally connected with your interest in seeing other Christians become great. Good Christians serve the Lord well. Great Christians serve him well and empower others to do the same.

Action Steps

1. Make a list of the significant people in your past who have had a positive influence on you. After each one's name, de-

scribe the characteristics that impacted you most. Which of their characteristics have become a part of your own character? Which ones are you ready to pass on to the next generation?

2. Write your own eulogy—what you would like people to say about you at your funeral. Then ask yourself if what you are doing now will result in the legacy you want to leave. If your current lifestyle is not likely to produce your desired legacy, develop a plan of action to invest your life more wisely for God's glory. Before this week is over, make the first lifestyle adjustment specified by your plan.

3. Memorize Mark 10:42–45:

> You know that those who are regarded as rulers of the Gentiles lord it over them, and their high officials exercise authority over them. Not so with you. Instead, whoever wants to become great among you must be your servant, and whoever wants to be first must be slave of all. For even the Son of Man did not come to be served, but to serve, and to give his life as a ransom for many.

Questions for Reflection and Discussion

1. In what ways have you tried to achieve greatness in the past? Did your attempts fit Jesus's definition of greatness or the world's? What were the results?

2. What evidence in a person's life would indicate that he or she is faithful? available? teachable? Do you demonstrate those qualities? Can you think of someone with those qualities whom God might want you to mentor?

3. How comfortable would you be in telling your children (or nieces and nephews) to watch your life carefully as they grow up so they can imitate your attitudes and behavior?

10

Develop Great Habits

Have you ever watched someone learning to play golf? The instructor shows the student how to position the hands on the club, how to bend the knees as the backswing begins, how to keep the front arm straight while the back arm bends, how to control the speed and angle of the club head, how to keep the eyes focused on the ball, how to accelerate the club on the downswing, how to shift body weight at the point of impact, and how to follow through—all in one fluid motion. Except when an aspiring golfer is taking beginner's lessons, the motion isn't fluid at all, is it? There's too much to remember, too many elements to concentrate on. The ball could fly in any direction because the movement is still awkward. The swing only seems natural and effortless when each element becomes automatic.

It's the same dynamic with almost anything we do. We make thousands of decisions a day, but we're not aware of most of them. They're automatic for us. We no longer need to remember each successive motion in tying a shoe, remind ourselves to brush our teeth every day, or deliberately check all the mirrors in the car. We have the ability to learn complex functions and then simplify them by frequent repetition until they become second nature. We tie our shoes without concentrating, brush our teeth without remembering for sure whether we did or not, and even drive home while talking on a cell phone, drinking a cup of coffee, and telling the children in the back seat to stop doing whatever they're doing. We accomplish a lot without thinking about our actions because, over time, we've developed habits.

We've talked about nine practices of great Christians in the previous chapters of this book, but those practices will just occupy space in your memory bank or a place on your bookshelf if one final practice doesn't integrate them into your life. Great Christians learn to live the Christian life in one fluid motion rather than an awkward series of movements because they've learned how to develop great habits.

By developing great habits, our other practices of dreaming great dreams, praying great prayers, and pursuing great people, for example, become part of a lifestyle rather than agenda items to check off. We unconsciously gravitate toward great people or enjoy great moments when we've incorporated the practices into our thinking and behavior. Like tying a shoe or brushing our teeth, these actions can become automatic. Habits are the thread that ties together the behaviors of great Christians in the Bible and church history.

The Power of Habits

Benjamin Franklin once said that if you take all your good habits and subtract all your bad habits, the result is your contribution to society. That's an interesting thought, isn't it? What we have been trained to do, whether good or bad, defines to some degree our benefit to the people around us—and to the kingdom of God.

Ted Pollock, an expert in time management and behavioral psychology, says that training yourself in good habits requires stern self-discipline at first. But once those habits become second nature, the payoff is considerable: "Good habits save effort, ease routines, increase efficiency, and release power."[1]

We need to grasp the fact that the sum of our good and bad habits will dictate who we will become. The kind of man or woman you will be in five, ten, or twenty years from now will be determined by the habits you have today. You can habitually learn to be kind, to think great thoughts, to be generous, to make great sacrifices, and so on. Those characteristics don't come accidentally. You have to cultivate a lifestyle in which those things can occur and become second nature.

This may sound more like a psychological technique than a scriptural imperative, but the Bible is clear that discipline is a godly means of grace. Spiritual growth and spiritual greatness come to us through our recurring practices. Habits create a framework that God fills with his grace. They become the highway on which grace is delivered.

In 1 Timothy, the apostle Paul writes to the young pastor Timothy, instructing him in his pastoral role. He encourages him not to be afraid but to exercise his gifts of leadership in spite of his youth. Then he tells Timothy to "have nothing to do with worldly fables." "On the other hand," he writes, "discipline yourself for the purpose of godliness" (1 Tim. 4:7 NASB). The word "discipline" can also be translated "practice" or "exercise." It's the same word we get *gymnasium* from, and it conveys the idea of going into training. And this is why it's important, Paul says: "Bodily discipline is only of little profit, but godliness is profitable for all things, since it holds promise for the present life and also for the life to come" (v. 8 NASB).

Godliness is profitable for eternity, Scripture says, and it comes in large part through discipline. In other words, when we approach our spiritual life like an athlete in training and develop the habits of godliness in the same manner that a weight lifter increases his strength, the consequences last forever. That's a lot of power to attribute to something as mundane—and often unappealing—as self-discipline.

In Hebrews, the writer addresses a group of Jewish Christians who are fading in their walk with the Lord. Persecution is intense, and they're shrinking back from their commitment to follow Jesus. After establishing the basis for believing in the supremacy of Christ, the writer reproves these believers:

It is hard to explain, since you have become dull of hearing. For though by this time you ought to be teachers, you have need again for someone to teach you the elementary principles of the oracles of God, and you have come to need milk and not solid food. For everyone who partakes only of milk is not accustomed to the word of righteousness, for he is an infant. But solid food is for the mature, who *because of practice have their senses trained* to discern good and evil.

Hebrews 5:11–14 NASB, emphasis added

Spiritual maturity, he says, belongs to those who have trained their senses.

Examining Your Habits

Each of us has routines we're generally unaware of. Some of us eat a snack before bedtime, watch a certain TV program each week, wake up to a certain preparation each morning, take vitamins, and so on. Our habits can be our best friends and our worst enemies. And when it comes to making a major lifestyle change, we can't just try to overlay our transformation on the same old habits. That won't work. If we want change, deeply ingrained habits need to be addressed.

One of my unconscious habits growing up was watching the eleven o'clock news before going to bed. Somehow I felt the world wasn't right until I knew what was going on in it. But you can't get up real early in the morning if you go to bed at 11:30. I realized that watching the news was not a profitable habit and that I could read the headlines the next morning. I could even save time by scanning only the stories that were really important rather than watching a whole program for a few interesting news bits. I decided to break my habit, and I've never regretted it. In fact, breaking that simple and seemingly harmless habit had a profound impact on my life.

At the same time I decided to stop watching the late-night news, I conducted a six-week experiment forbidding my kids from watching TV on school nights. For two or three days, it was bedlam. Everyone got on each other's nerves. But by the fourth day, we were playing games together. The next week, the kids were playing the guitar or working on various projects. Some nights we worked outside together. We'd have a great family time, and then at nine o'clock we'd be tired and ready to go to bed. When you're going to bed that early every night, it's pretty easy to get up earlier in the morning. I gained two and a half hours in my day, and it changed my entire schedule. People tell me today that I juggle a lot of balls, and maybe that's true. But if I do, it's because more than twenty years ago, God gave me back over two hours each day. And my kids developed their musical talents, read a lot of great books, explored their creative impulses, and built great relationships in the family because we changed one particular practice. That's the power of a habit.

Habits that Cultivate Grace

Titus 2:11–12 tells us that it's the grace of God that teaches us "to deny ungodliness and worldly desires and to live sensibly, righteously and godly in the present age" (NASB). So often we pit grace and effort in opposition against each other, but that's not scriptural. Grace and effort go hand in hand. Grace and *merit* stand opposed to each other; the idea of earning God's favor is called legalism. But the gospel doesn't teach that we don't exert effort to be obedient and faithful. In fact, we are commanded to "make every effort" to live with one another in humility and unity (Eph. 4:3). God's grace gives us both the desire and the ability to be righteous and follow him. Godliness only comes through grace, but it takes great effort to apply grace fully to our lives.

With that in mind, let's look at six habits that help cultivate your experience of grace. Think of these habits not as ways to earn God's approval, but as spiritual pipelines that allow God's grace to transform your life. God will use them to pour his unmerited favor into your heart and mind so that by his power you can become more and more like Christ.

1. Put God First

This is the *principle of priority* expressed in Matthew 6:33: "Seek first his kingdom and his righteousness, and all these things will be given to you as well." Develop the habit of giving God the first portion and the best part of your day.

Good Christians, of course, can meet with God any time they want—morning, noon, or night. They're in the Bible, praying, and meeting with God on a semiregular basis. But great Christians give their first and best time to meet with God before anything else. Throughout church history and quite often in Scripture, this means those morning hours when we are fresh and know with relative certainty that nothing can interfere with our time with God. For some, a different time of day may better suit them. But I've found that carving out the first portion of the day has helped me become far more consistent in my time with God and carries much less potential for emergencies and interruptions. If you've tried to spend consistent time with God and have been unsuccessful, let me suggest that you try the morning hours—even if you're not a morning person. Try buying an alarm clock without a snooze button. That's a battle you can win; it's "mind over mattress."

More important than the time of day, however, is the attitude that drives you into God's presence. Great Christians thirst for God like a deer pants for water (Ps. 42:1–2), and they wait for him more than a watchman waits for the morning (Ps. 130:6). When you study the lives of great men and women, as well as the psychology of forming habits, you discover that people find a way to prioritize what matters most to them.

Carving out a regular morning quiet time was the most difficult habit I've ever established. In my early years, my normal way of getting up was to hit the snooze button whenever the alarm went off—once, twice, three times . . . as often as I could until about five minutes before class time. You can get away with that in college. Just throw on some sweat pants and a sweatshirt, run as fast as you can, and get there only a few minutes late. When someone taught me how to have a quiet time, I constantly struggled with consistency. I'd work only about fifteen minutes in, maybe twice a week.

For me, this wasn't an issue of being legalistic; I really wanted to establish a regular time to meet and enjoy God. I could always convince myself at night that I would get up on time the next morning, but I could always convince myself the next morning that I'd start some other day. So to make myself get up when the alarm clock rang, I put it on the other side of the room. But even that didn't work. I had an amazing ability to get up, turn it off, and go right back to bed.

Finally, I called in the special forces. Bob was a heavyweight wrestler, self-disciplined, and my college roommate. So I asked him to help me. Surely he would be a little more difficult to ignore than an alarm clock.

"Are you sure you want to get up no matter what?" he asked.

"Yes, whatever it takes," I assured him. The next morning when the alarm went off, I hit the snooze button as usual.

"Chip, it's time."

"Oh, just forget it," I mumbled. "We can start tomorrow."

"Remember, Chip, this wasn't my idea. You asked me, and I promised I'd get you up."

"I know. Don't worry about it. It's okay."

But Bob was a man of his word. He went to the end of my bed, grabbed my ankle, picked me up—upside down—and started carrying me to the bathroom.

"Bob, put me down! What are you doing?"

"You want to learn to get up?"

"Yeah."

"You want to meet with God?"

"Yeah."

"Okay, you asked for it." Then he opened the door to the shower and made sure I wouldn't be comfortable going straight back to bed.

Bob repeated his technique for a few days until I caught on. It was radical, but it worked. Some habits require drastic measures, but if you're serious about putting God first, you'll be willing to do whatever it takes. I eventually learned to get up on my own, and I spent time with God at least five mornings a week. Sometimes it felt like duty, but when you know something is right, you do it anyway.

I wish I could tell you amazing stories about how the skies opened and the words of Scripture jumped right off the page and into my heart, but I can't. Of course, I had some great times with God, but it wasn't necessarily an "emotional high" each morning. It's like breakfast; I don't always remember what I ate, but it does a lot of good for my body. Over the months that followed, my time with God went from fifteen to thirty minutes, and it went from duty to delight—not every single time, of course, but more often than not, and it kept me motivated. I stopped dreading it and started looking forward to it like it was a date with my wife or a meal at my favorite restaurant. At some point in the years following, I quit setting alarms and asked God to wake me up whenever he wanted to. Sometimes the first hour or two of my day are the best and most satisfying. If I had to point to one habit that has transformed my life more than any other, it would be getting up to spend time with God.

2. Take Out the Trash

The *principle of transformation* comes straight out of Romans 12:2: "Do not be conformed to this world, but be transformed by the renewing of your mind, so that you may prove what the will of God is, that which is good and acceptable and perfect" (NASB). There's a negative command in that verse that literally says to stop being conformed, or molded, to this world. Quit allowing the world system—its ideas, images, and values—to shape who you are. Get the trash out of your life.

That's followed by a positive command to allow God's Word to renew and transform you—to cause a *metamorphosis*, the same word used for the transfiguration of Jesus. Grammatically, this command is in the passive voice; God does it, but we allow it. We let our minds be transformed from the inside out so we can be people who prove and experience the will of God. Our lifestyle begins to demonstrate God's will—that which is good and acceptable and perfect.

In my first pastorate in Kaufman, Texas, an older man who looked like he'd been through a lot came to church. His shirt was dirty, he looked and smelled like he hadn't taken a bath in six months, and he was hungry. We gave him some food, and the next week he brought his wife, who was in just as bad a condition as he was. After the service, they said they needed some money for electricity and other necessities.

The church had a fund to help people, so I offered to go out to their house and visit. Theresa and I drove out in the country and found a house that didn't look very bad at all. A couple of horses and about five or six dogs in the yard all looked pretty healthy. But when we entered the house, I almost threw up from the stench. Garbage was on the floor, a container of something that had spoiled was left open, and cans of cat food for the nineteen cats running around the kitchen were spread out everywhere. The shades were pulled down, and he, his wife, and a very elderly woman sat in near darkness. I wondered how they could tolerate such nasty conditions, but when people live around trash long enough, they get accustomed to it. It starts to seem normal. We get used to a nauseating stench if we breathe it long enough.

Spiritually, a lot of Christians have filled their minds with so much garbage from the junkyard of this world that it doesn't seem like garbage anymore. Their lives never change, and they can't figure out why. The things that God has called "trash"—unholy attitudes and behaviors, unrighteousness, choices that will lead us down a bad path and ruin our relationships—have become very acceptable among many believers. We're often trying to figure out what's true and righteous when God has already told us how to find out. He has given us his Word to guide us and put his Spirit within us. If we don't quench the Spirit, our conscience will lead us in the right direction. But if we choose to live in squalor, we'll start to accept it as normal.

This is why many polls report almost identical statistics between Christians and non-Christians on issues like marital fidelity, honesty, spending habits, and addiction to pornography. We're unconsciously being conformed to this world, not transformed to the image of Christ. We eat and drink what the world offers us in enticing advertisements, standards of living, romance novels and soap operas, Internet porn, violent movies and video games, and so much more simply because we haven't consciously determined to stop being conformed to "the pattern of this world" (Rom. 12:2). The result is impure thoughts and attitudes that build a nest in our hearts and minds. The world system is so seductive that sometimes we just have to stop and separate ourselves from it for a few days or weeks.

Every so often, I sense that I'm being so pulled by the world system that I take a media fast for an extended period of time. For a week or ten days—sometimes longer—I don't watch TV or videos or listen to news or talk radio. Then when I come off my media fast, I'm always shocked by what I see on TV. Try it sometime. When you take a break from garbage, it will smell like garbage when you return. Things you hardly noticed before will suddenly appear blatantly sinful and distasteful.

As a pastor, let me ask you a sensitive question about your spiritual health: What trash do you have in your life right now? If Jesus were inside your mind today and you asked him what he thought about its contents, which areas would he find most uncomfortable? He wouldn't condemn you for it; he still loves you just the same. But would he feel at home there? The point of Romans 12:1–2 is not to condemn but to bless you with the experience of God's perfect will by the renewing of your mind. Which areas of your life need to have some trash taken out?

3. Do Your Own Dishes

The *principle of responsibility* takes the blame off of other people and forces us to be accountable for our own messes. Too many people make excuses for the way they are or for what they've done: "It's my parents' fault." "The system let me down." "My boss is unreasonable." "The government isn't fair. . . ." It can get a lot more elaborate than that, too: "Maybe I was going a little too fast, but I had to keep up with the flow of traffic, right? And it wouldn't have happened if he'd turned on his signal a second earlier, because then I'd have had time to slam on the brakes. Besides, someone going that slow is a danger to everyone else on the road. If anyone should be at fault, it should be him. . . ."

People who have a performance-based relationship with God don't understand or accept the fullness of his grace, and they develop a habit of making excuses and blaming people or circumstances for everything that goes wrong—even when they've contributed to the problem themselves. When we do that, we don't change.

When we were young, many of us had mothers who always did the dishes for us, no matter how busy their schedule or how tiring their day. They would get up first and go to bed last because of all the cleanup they had to do around the rest of us. Do you know what many of them were thinking? "I have so much to do; I can't believe they don't realize how this affects my day. Do they think there are dish fairies that come along and clean all this up?"

We usually don't make a conscious decision to expect others to clean up our messes. It's a habit. But behind that habit is an assumption that it's up to someone else to make our life work.

It is our spiritual responsibility before God to clean up our own dishes. Don't pile all difficulties in other people's sinks for them to deal with. Jesus gave us a timeless axiom about responsibility in a passage about finances: "He who is faithful in a very little thing is faithful in much; and he who is unrighteous in a very little thing is unrighteous also in much" (Luke 16:10 NASB). The point is that personal responsibility extends to even the smallest details. Until we learn to own up to our obligations, we won't be faithful in the larger issues of the kingdom of God.

I learned this lesson during a summer ministry with a para-. church organization. A group of us went to a large city to get some much-needed ministry experience. We roomed together in a sorority house, got day jobs, and spent our evenings in evangelism. We took "faith trips" out into the community to find people we could serve and love. On one of those trips, our team of five guys stopped at a gas station that wasn't very nice. We each went to the dirty restroom, and as I was washing my hands I noticed John, our team leader, coming out of the stall. He pulled off some toilet paper and wiped the seat down. After he washed his hands, he grabbed a couple extra paper towels, wiped off the sink, and even picked up some of the junk people had dropped on the floor. The whole routine only took about fifteen or twenty seconds, but I couldn't believe he even took that much time to clean up behind people who clearly didn't give a rip about cleanliness.

"You looking for a little janitorial work, John?" I asked. I could be rather sarcastic back then.

He stopped and looked at me very seriously. "No, Chip, not at all," he said. "A disciple of Jesus Christ always leaves everything better than he found it. Someone is going to sit on that seat later. Someone's going to wash his hands in that sink. I don't know them, but I don't need to. I just need to serve them. If Jesus were here, he would want something better for them. If I owned this gas station and someone left paper all over the floor, I'd certainly want someone to pick it up for the next people coming in."

I had never thought of that. It was an immediate paradigm shift for me. John taught me that Christians not only do their own dishes, they do them for other people too. You take responsibility for your life, your actions, your choices, and your messes; but then you go beyond that and help others with theirs. I've never forgotten that lesson, and it still impacts me today. When I borrow a car, I return it clean and full of gas. When I get something out of the refrigerator, I put it back. When I take clothes off, I hang them up. An amazing number of marital problems are solved by this principle. So are many relational conflicts we have with other people.

How does that begin? With a habit. Early in our marriage, after my wife had worked hard all day to wash, dry, iron, and fold the clothes, I'd come in with my mind full of "more important" things, take all the clothes she'd folded and put on the bed, and stack them on a dresser where they'd sit for three or four days until I put them away. You know what that communicated to her? "I know you worked hard to do all this, but it isn't very important to me." That's not the message I intended to send, obviously, but it's the message she got. The only way to break that habit was to start a new one. It wasn't very complicated. When I come in and my laundry has been done, I put it away immediately. It's as easy to do right away as it is three days later. All it takes is a new habit.

That's a household example of a broad, spiritual truth. When you take responsibility for yourself, you cultivate habits of being kind, being faithful, being a good steward, and looking out for the needs of others. You're accountable for your messes, your future, your money, and your relationships. By God's grace, culti-vate the habit of not expecting anyone else to do your dishes.

4. Write It Down

The *principle of clarity* can be found in Proverbs 20:5: "A plan in the heart of a man is like deep water, but a man of under-standing draws it out" (NASB). We all have plans, dreams, and purposes embedded deep within our hearts. For many, those plans stay beneath the surface for a lifetime, but an understand-ing person "draws [them] out." God uses others to ask prob-ing questions, provide insights, and help us to discover these plans. Sometimes, however, those people aren't available when something is brewing in our heart or when we need a way to process what God is doing in us. Though there's no substitute for godly counsel, I've learned that writing my thoughts in a journal and expressing key issues, goals, and feelings on paper can help me "draw out" the plans God has put within me. The "deep water" of the heart often isn't clear until I do.

We have a lot of questions in this complex world: Where should I send my kids to school? Should I respond to this person now or wait and give God time to work? How do I know when to ditch plan A and start on plan B? The first three principles in this chapter—putting God first, getting the garbage out, and tak-ing responsibility—are great first steps for navigating through the complexity of life. But once you've done that, how do you proactively move forward? I've found that writing things down has a surprisingly powerful effect. Let me offer some specific examples that have been helpful to me.

Three-by-five cards. A friend named Bill shared with me *the power of clear-cut objectives*. He would write his specific desires and goals on three-by-five cards. "I don't try to memorize them," he said. "I just keep them out there so my mind and my heart can gravitate toward them." That was twenty years ago, and I've been doing it ever since. I began with the things I knew for certain:

> I want to be a man of God and walk before God in integrity all the days of my life.

> I want to demonstrate love for Theresa in a way that makes sense to her each day in some specific way.

> I would like to help each of my children discover their spiritual gifts and God's will for their life.

> I want to work out on a regular basis and not feel guilty about it so I can stay in good shape.

> I would like to pray for extended times and learn to become habitually thankful for all things.

I followed Bill's example and read my cards each morning and evening for about a month and then two or three times a week afterward. Over time, a lot of things became clear: this is how I want to live; this is where I want to go; this is what I want to do; here's the kind of man I want to be. When you write down your life goals and the desires of your heart, you will unconsciously gravitate toward them. That's the way our minds work. When I decide it's time to buy a new car and settle on the model I'd like, they start showing up everywhere on the road. They were always there, but I didn't notice them because I didn't have a clear goal. In the same way, when we write down our plans and dreams, we begin to be pulled in those directions. The power of clear-cut objectives draws us toward them.

Calendars. I hate calendars. I'm a spontaneous, undisciplined person by nature, and calendars give the impression of hemming me in. All any of us really want is to do whatever we want to do whenever we want to do it. But I've found that instead of confining me to a schedule, calendars actually offer me *the freedom of structure.*

Years ago I had an *ah-hah* moment when I realized that my to-do list never ends. No matter how busy we are accomplishing the items on those lists, they just get longer and longer, don't they? We keep adding to them. I had to ask myself whether I wanted to be a doer or a be-er, and the answer was clear that Jesus is focused on who we are more than what we do. Both are important, but *doing* comes out of *being*, not vice versa. I realized that I would never be the kind of person God wanted me to be if I was always doing what I assumed he or other people wanted me to do. So I took my good desires from my three-by-five cards and put them on my calendar first. I wanted a great marriage, so I wrote down a date with Theresa on every Friday. I wanted to be a great dad, so I blocked off calendar time with my kids. Same with staying in shape, prayer time, and so on. All of my *be* items went on the calendar before my *do* items. Then all the phone calls and important meetings had to fit in around them.

Do you know what that does? No, it still doesn't get everything done on the to-do list. If you're looking for that moment when you're completely caught up with every task you ever wanted and needed to do, this isn't going to get you there. (And I don't know anything else that will.) But if you're looking for a way to direct the course of your life, this will help you like it has helped me. It isn't very dramatic and it doesn't sound very spiritual, but for over twenty years I've had a regular date with my wife, I've been working out three or four times a week, I've prayed consistently, and so on. Over time, I've stayed healthy and built a great relationship with my family—and with God. Major breakthroughs are great, but much of life revolves around consistency in the minor details. You can be the person you envision being if you identify the steps you need to take, learn how to prioritize them, and then actually *do* them. Huge areas of your life can prosper, all because a few important practices were given some structure on a calendar.

To-do lists. I know, I just got through saying they never get done. But they're still important because they help us with *the necessity of focus.* Write your responsibilities and opportunities down at the beginning of the week and put a star by the essentials: the ones that you really want to do, the ones that will get you in trouble if you don't do, and the ones that will have the greatest impact. Then ask God for help with each one. As each item is completed, cross it off your list and thank God for his help. What looks like only an itemized agenda to most people can actually become a very spiritual tool. Your to-do list can become a prayer guide for your personal needs. It reminds you not only what you have to do but what you need God's help with—and then it provides evidence of his faithfulness as you meet your daily responsibilities. Your weekly agenda can become much more manageable and enjoyable when you've invited the power of God into it.

Journals. Writing your prayers, thoughts, circumstances, fears, hopes, and dreams in a journal satisfies *the need for reflection*. A journal is a great place to be completely honest with God. I've got hundreds of entries that start with truthful complaints: "Lord, I'm really tired today. I feel really overwhelmed. I don't know how I'm going to do it. I've got six things on my mind, and somewhere underneath that I feel angry, but I don't know why. I'll just keep writing until you show me. And about that dream on my heart, last night I was thinking about this, and I don't know if you'd ever allow me to do it, but would you . . . ?" As you begin to reflect on whatever's going on inside of you, the deep purposes of the heart start to get drawn out. Writing in a journal takes away the busyness of nonstop going and doing and gives you time to speak to God and him to speak to you—heart to heart.

5. Do It Now

A lot of things never get done because we never get started doing them. That's the *principle of inertia*. There's tremendous power in actually starting something.

Proverbs 24:30–34 (NASB) says:

> I passed by the field of the sluggard
>   And by the vineyard of the man lacking sense,
> And behold, it was completely overgrown with thistles;
>   Its surface was covered with nettles,
>   And its stone wall was broken down.
> When I saw, I reflected upon it;
>   I looked, and received instruction.
> "A little sleep, a little slumber,
>   A little folding of the hands to rest,"
> Then your poverty will come as a robber
>   And your want like an armed man.

Thistles, nettles, and broken walls are signs of neglect. The lazy person leaves plenty of evidence that nothing has been done. When the author of this proverbial picture saw this scene, he "received instruction"—God often uses everyday sights as teaching opportunities—and the lesson he learned was that a little procrastination can do a lot of damage. When we decide to discipline the kids later or pay the bills some other time, the consequences can be surprisingly sudden and overwhelming. Most of us live a life full of good intentions and broken promises. We intend to do this new project or establish that new practice, but it never quite happens.

Learn to attack life. Whatever it is, do it now. Include enjoying great moments into your plan of attack; "do it now" applies even to rest and recreation, not just your to-do list. But quit postponing difficult tasks. Have that unpleasant conversation now. Whatever you dread most, get it over with early in the day.

That's how I made it through Greek and Hebrew study in seminary. I had to get up at four in the morning because if I didn't get language homework done by seven, when I had to catch my carpool, I knew I wouldn't have the motivation or the discipline in me later. I had a wife and kids and a job—and no desire to neglect them at the expense of learning languages that looked like chicken scratchings at the time. I'm glad I learned that stuff now, but it didn't come easy for me. I had to block off a couple of early morning hours at an all-night coffee shop, because if I didn't do it "now," it wouldn't get done.

When you cultivate habits that get the small things and the hard things done before you have time to dread them, it benefits the rest of your life. Obligations don't pile up and weigh heavily on your shoulders, sapping energy and motivation from you because you know they still need to be done. When you've procrastinated and have a week's worth of papers to file, twelve calls to return, several days' worth of homework or office projects to complete, and five loads of laundry to do, it's a little demotivating, isn't it? All of life feels discouraging and depressing with too many responsibilities hanging over your head. And when we're depressed, all many of us want to do is watch TV and eat—not exactly problem-solving activities. That approach actually creates habits of facing difficulties in passive, negligent ways. Try playing that out for a decade or two and see how wonderful life gets. It won't be pretty. Attack life by doing today's work today, and you'll feel a lot better about tomorrow.

6. Turn It Off

This is the *principle of restoration*—a thoroughly biblical command. "There remains a Sabbath rest for the people of God. For the one who has entered His rest has himself rested from his works, as God did from His. Therefore let us be diligent to enter that rest, so that no one will fall, through following the same example of disobedience" (Heb. 4:9–11 NASB).

Did you notice the irony? We have to "be diligent" to "enter that rest." Why? Because rest doesn't come easily for us. For those who already have a "do it now" mentality, the biblical practice of keeping a Sabbath offers a much-needed balance. Yes, we're to do our work proactively and not procrastinate. But we still need to turn off the cell phone and the computer and take a break. We have to be diligent to cut off the conditions that keep us from resting.

This is a huge faith issue. All of your business competitors may be producing goods and earning money seven days a week, and it makes perfect sense that you'll lose out by closing down one day a week. But in God's economy, he gets to define what makes sense. And he promises that those who trust him and obey him will be taken care of. He'll see to that. One example is Chick-fil-A, a restaurant that in spite of changes in business and culture over the last few decades has continued to remain closed every Sunday. It's thriving anyway; God clearly hasn't let that company down.

The Sabbath, Jesus said, is God's gift. In Colossians 2 we learn that the New Testament believers were concerned more with the principle than the uniform practice, but they still applied the principle diligently. You may need to establish a different day of rest than other people practice, but the important thing is to do it. Close the calendar, turn off the phones and pagers, shut the computers down, and look back on your week in grati-

tude. Enjoy his creation with the people you love. Spend some
extra time with him. You don't have to be legalistic about it; if
an emergency comes up, deal with it. But make up for it later.
Honor the day of rest God gives you.

This practice saved my life years ago. As a recovering workaholic, I had to learn that there's a huge difference between having drive and being driven. The only way to break unhealthy
work patterns was to make myself stop. I developed a habit of
leaving work at the office and going home to be the husband,
father, and child of God I needed to be. That may be as hard
for some of you as it was for me, but you can't be the man or
woman God intends if you're on call all the time. Take twenty-
four hours every seven days and simply stop. Be restored, renewed, and refreshed. How? Whatever "it" is, turn it off.[2]

Some Practical Steps

To keep you going on the path of greatness, I encourage
you to identify the one bad habit you've never gotten rid of
and that you are most convinced will come back to bite you.
Write it on a sheet of paper and tell yourself that it has to be
broken. Then ask God which one of the six good habits in this
chapter he wants you to develop first. Sit quietly and let him
highlight one of them for you. Then find someone to help keep
you accountable, come up with a plan, don't get discouraged
with setbacks—habits can take a long time to form and a long
time to break—and begin to arrange your life accordingly. Set
yourself up to break your most difficult habit and establish
your most needed habit.

Once you've done that, you've trained yourself in the processes of habit breaking and habit forming. You can do it again
and again, taking each area of your life and rearranging it.
You'll be able to incorporate all the practices we've discussed
in this book and many more. You'll find yourself moving from
frustration to fruitfulness and from resignation to resolve. And
you will be on an exciting path from good to great—in God's
eyes.

Action Steps

1. Identify one habit that you know God wants you to change. Set a specific goal for this week—a first step in breaking that habit and establishing a new one in its place—that is achievable and measurable. Enlist one accountability partner and give that person permission to hold you to your goal and ask you about it frequently. Then repeat the process for the next step of habit breaking and habit forming.

2. Make a list of your ultimate goals in life, prioritize them, and then break them down into manageable steps. For example, if one of your goals is to have a great marriage, determine the priority it ought to receive and then identify the habits that will accomplish it (such as counseling, regular date nights, etc.). Put your manageable steps on a calendar or a to-do list, and then *follow through on it.* (Coming up with a plan and implementing it are two different things. Most people excel at stage one but fail at stage two. Don't be one of them.)

3. In your quiet times with God this week, write down your prayers, dreams, desires, worries, and so on. At the end of the week, read through them and ask God to help you "draw out" his plans for you.

4. Memorize Romans 12:2, "Do not be conformed to this world, but be transformed by the renewing of your mind, so that you may prove what the will of God is, that which is good and acceptable and perfect" (NASB).

Questions for Reflection and Discussion

1. When you consider your spiritual growth, are you more likely to look for major breakthroughs or consistent habits? Which has God used most powerfully in your life? Why do you think both are important?

2. How drastically would your lifestyle change if you went on a temporary media fast? What spiritual benefits would you expect to experience?

3. If you asked God which of your habits he'd most like to change, what do you think he would say? Which habit do you think pleases him the most? What steps can you take right now to break your worst habit and cultivate your best habit? Can you think of someone who will help you be accountable for both?

Notes

Introduction

1. Jim Collins, *Good to Great: Why Some Companies Make the Leap—and Others Don't* (New York: HarperBusiness, 2001).

Chapter 1 Think Great Thoughts

1. See, for example, Jack B. Haskins and Alice Kendrick, *Successful Advertising Research Methods* (Lincolnwood, IL: NTC Business Books, 1993).

2. Henry Varley, 1872, quoted by J. Gilchrist Lawson, "D. L. Moody," Christian Biography Resources, on the Wholesome Words website, http://www.wholesomewords .org/biography/biomoody4.html.

3. John Stott, *Only One Way: The Message of Galatians* (London: Inter-Varsity, 1968), 170.

4. Charles H. Spurgeon, *An All-Round Ministry: Addresses to Ministers and Students* (repr.; Pasadena, TX: Pilgrim Publications, 1983), 124, http://www.spurgeon .org/misc/aarm04.htm.

Chapter 2 Read Great Books

1. A. W. Tozer, *The Knowledge of the Holy* (San Francisco: HarperSanFrancisco, 1978), 1.

2. Ibid., 83.

3. Betty Lee Skinner, *Daws: The Story of Dawson Trotman, Founder of the Navigators* (Grand Rapids: Zondervan, 1974).

4. James Hefley and Marti Hefley, *Uncle Cam: The Story of William Cameron Townsend, Founder of the Wycliffe Bible Translators and the Summer Institute of Linguistics*, photo editor, Cornell Capa (Waco: Word, 1974).

5. Statistics for Wycliffe participation in Bible translation current as of 2006, released by International Corporate Communications, March 2007, Wycliffe International, http://www.wycliffe.net/v2025.shtml (accessed March 30, 2007).

6. Dr. and Mrs. Howard Taylor, *Hudson Taylor's Spiritual Secret* (London: China Inland Mission, 1932).

7. Jay E. Adams, *How to Overcome Evil* (Phillipsburg, NJ: Presbyterian and Reformed, 1977).

8. Francis Schaeffer, *Escape from Reason* (London: Inter-Varsity Fellowship, 1968); Francis Schaeffer, *The God Who Is There* (Downers Grove, IL: InterVarsity Press, 1998); Francis Schaeffer, *He Is There and He Is Not Silent* (Wheaton: Tyndale, 1972).

9. Francis Schaeffer, *True Spirituality* (Wheaton: Tyndale, 1971).

10. E. M. Bounds, *Power Through Prayer* (Grand Rapids: Zondervan, 1962); Andrew Murray, *Humility: The Beauty of Holiness* (Fort Washington, PA: Christian Literature Crusade, 1997); Roy Hession, *My Calvary Road* (Grand Rapids: Zondervan, 1978).

11. Evelyn Christenson and Viola Blake, *What Happens When Women Pray* (Wheaton: Victor Books, 1975).

12. Bounds, Power Through Prayer, 12.

13. Larry Christenson, *The Christian Family* (Minneapolis: Bethany Fellowship, 1974).

14. H. Norman Wright, *Communication: Key to Your Marriage: Practical, Biblical Ways to Improve Communication and Enrich Your Marriage*, ed. Fritz Ridenour (Glendale, CA: Regal Books, 1974).

15. David Stoop and Jan Stoop, *The Intimacy Factor* (Nashville: Nelson, 1993).

16. Peter Drucker, *The Effective Executive* (New York: Harper & Row, 1967).

17. Charles Ryrie, *Basic Theology* (Wheaton: Victor Books, 1986); J. Sidlow Baxter, *Explore the Book* (Grand Rapids: Zondervan, 1960); Robert Traina, *Methodical Bible Study: A New Approach to Hermeneutics* (New York: Biblical Seminary in New York, 1952).

18. Paul Tournier, *The Strong and the Weak*, trans. Edwin Hudson (Philadelphia: Westminster Press, 1963).

19. Henri Nouwen, *The Return of the Prodigal Son: A Story of Homecoming* (New York: Image, 1993).

20. Brennan Manning, *Abba's Child: The Cry of the Heart for Intimate Belonging* (Colorado Springs: NavPress, 1994).

Chapter 3 Pursue Great People

1. In 2 Kings 2:10, Elijah says, "If you see me when I am taken from you, it will be yours." The Hebrew text (and context) of that verse seems to imply *watching*—active, intentional gazing—rather than passively noticing whether Elijah was visible.

Chapter 4 Dream Great Dreams

1. Jim Collins and Jerry I. Porras, *Built to Last: Successful Habits of Visionary Companies* (New York: HarperBusiness, 1994).

2. Dietrich Bonhoeffer, *The Cost of Discipleship*, trans. R. H. Fuller (London: SCM Press, 1948).

Chapter 5 Pray Great Prayers

1. Francis McGaw, *John Hyde: Apostle of Prayer* (Minneapolis: Bethany, 1986).

Chapter 8 Enjoy Great Moments

1. C. S. Lewis, *Letters to Malcolm: Chiefly on Prayer* (New York: Harcourt, Brace & World, 1964), 92–93.

2. Jonathan Edwards, "The Spirit of Love the Opposite of a Selfish Spirit," sermon 8 in *Charity and Its Fruits: Christian Love as Manifested in the Heart and Life*, ed. Tryon Edwards (London: Banner of Truth Trust, 1969), 159.

3. C. S. Lewis, *The Weight of Glory and Other Addresses* (San Francisco: Harper-SanFrancisco, 2001), 26.

4. Dallas Willard's counsel, mentioned in John Ortberg, *The Life You've Always Wanted: Spiritual Disciplines for Ordinary People* (Grand Rapids: Zondervan, 1997), 81.

5. Dallas Willard, *The Spirit of the Disciplines* (San Francisco: HarperSanFrancisco, 1988).

Chapter 9 Empower Great People

1. C. J. Mahaney, *Humility: True Greatness* (Sisters, OR: Multnomah, 2005), 44.

2. Example of 2 Timothy 2:2, given by Dawson Trotman, "Spiritual Reproduction," audio tape (n.d.).

3. Brian O'Reilly, "Why Grade 'A' Execs Get an 'F' as Parents," *Fortune*, January 1, 1990, 36–46.

Chapter 10 Develop Great Habits

1. Ted Pollock, quoted in "Increase Your Self-Discipline," *Executive Leadership*, National Institute of Business Management (2007), 6, http://www.exec-leadership.com/sample/sampleissue.pdf.

2. For those who need some help with this one, I highly recommend Mark Buchanan's *The Rest of God: Restoring Your Soul by Restoring Sabbath* (Nashville: W Publishing Group, 2006).

Chip Ingram is the president and teaching pastor for *Living on the Edge*, an international teaching and discipleship ministry. His passion is to help everyday Christians actually "live like Christians" by raising the bar of discipleship. A pastor for over twenty years, Chip has a unique ability to communicate truth and winsomely challenge people to live out their faith. Chip is the author of nine books, including *Effective Parenting in a Defective World*; *God: As He Longs for You to See Him*; *Love, Sex, and Lasting Relationships*; *The Miracle of Life Change*; *Holy Ambition*; and *The Invisible War*. Chip and his wife, Theresa, have four children and six grandchildren.

For more information about Chip Ingram or *Living on the Edge*, please visit www.lote.org.

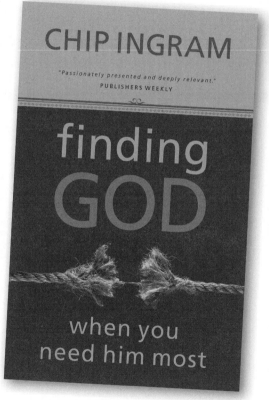

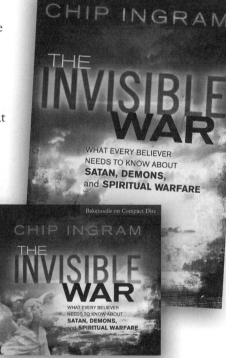

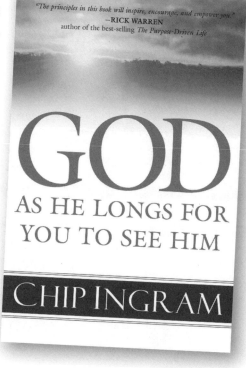

LIVING ON THE EDGE
community

DISCOVER THE TOOLS YOU NEED TO DEEPEN YOUR RELATIONSHIP WITH GOD

Get plugged into:

- *Proven pathways of discipleship*

- *Hear relevant messages*

- *Read thought-provoking articles*

- *Ask questions, and more*

Let us help you take your next steps with God.

You are not alone on your journey.

LOG ON NOW...
...to discover how the Community can help you grow.

www.lote.org/community